THE
HORSE
LOVER

A Cowboy's Quest to Save

the Wild Mustangs

H. ALAN DAY

With Lynn Wiese Sneyd

Foreword by Sandra Day O'Connor

University of Nebraska Press | Lincoln and London

Some names in this account have been
changed to protect people's privacy.

Publication of this volume was assisted
by a grant from the Friends of the
University of Nebraska Press.

Library of Congress
Cataloging-in-Publication Data
Day, H. Alan.
The horse lover: a cowboy's quest to save the wild
mustangs / H. Alan Day with Lynn Wiese Sneyd;
foreword by Sandra Day O'Connor.   pages cm
ISBN 978-0-8032-5335-3 (cloth: alkaline paper) —
ISBN 978-0-8032-5500-5 (epub) — ISBN 978-0-8032-
5501-2 (mobi) — ISBN 978-0-8032-5499-2 (pdf)
1. Mustang—Conservation—South Dakota.
2. Wild horses—Conservation—South
Dakota. 3. Day, H. Alan. 4. Cowboys—
South Dakota—Biography. 5. Ranchers—South
Dakota—Biography. 6. Wildlife conservationists—
South Dakota—Biography. 7. Wild
horses—Government policy—United States.
8. Mustang—Government policy—United
States. 9. Ranch life—South Dakota. 10. South
Dakota—Social life and customs. I. Sneyd, Lynn
Wiese. II. O'Connor, Sandra Day, 1930–. III. Title.
SF293.M9D39 2014
599.665'5—dc23   2013035591

Set in Dante by Laura Wellington.
Designed by Nathan Putens.

This book is dedicated to fellow horse lovers everywhere.

Be it enacted by the Senate and House of Representatives of the United States of America in Congress assembled, That Congress finds and declares that wild free-roaming horses and burros are living symbols of the historic and pioneer spirit of the West; that they contribute to the diversity of life forms within the Nation and enrich the lives of the American people; and that these horses and burros are fast disappearing from the American scene. It is the policy of Congress that wild free-roaming horses and burros shall be protected from capture, branding, harassment, or death; and to accomplish this they are to be considered in the area where presently found, as an integral part of the natural system of the public lands.
— *The Wild and Free-Roaming Horses and Burros Act of 1971*

There is something about the outside of a horse
that is good for the inside of a man.
— *Winston Churchill*

Contents

Illustrations

Foreword

When my brother, Alan, told me that he had agreed to keep fifteen hundred wild mustangs on his South Dakota ranch, I thought he had temporarily lost his common sense. It sounded like a very challenging task and a great deal harder than raising cattle, which he knew how to do very well. Indeed, Alan had been a cattle rancher all his adult life. But Alan was very enthusiastic about the mustang project and about seeing whether he and the mustangs could adjust to each other. Alan likes a challenge and the project was certainly that.

For more than four hundred years, wild mustangs have existed in the region that is now the western United States. They fared well before the Taylor Grazing Act of 1934 reduced their habitat. But even in the last century there were many pockets of public land in the West where they could live free, breed, and multiply. But the pressures of the multiple-use policy of the Bureau of Land Management and the restricted uses of national forest and national park lands meant that many of the wild mustangs would be captured, sold, or destroyed. The wild horse and burro law dictated that the Bureau of Land Management was to capture many of them and care for them until they could be adopted. Sadly, many of them were not suitable for adoption. This opened the way for the project Alan undertook.

It is impossible to see a herd of wild horses running free without feeling a surge of excitement and enthusiasm for their vigor, power, and beauty. To watch them run with their manes and tails flying in the wind is to experience a sense of the ultimate freedom of motion.

This book tells the story of the Mustang Meadows project in a way that enables the reader to see and feel that excitement and to glimpse what was and what might have been with these splendid animals.

Sandra Day O'Connor

Acknowledgments

Few books come to fruition without teamwork, and we were fortunate to gather and work with an exceptionally talented team. A special thank you to Sandra Day O'Connor for encouragement that began long before the first draft even emerged and continued throughout the writing process. Stuart Krichevsky's guiding wisdom early on kept us focused on a story about horses, horses, horses. Matt Bokovoy of the University of Nebraska Press grabbed this project and, along with Martyn Beeny and the rest of the folks at that fine organization, poured unending energy, vision, and support into it. We also were blessed to have the eyes and editing talents of Liza Wiemer, Meg Files, Nancy Wiese, Marina Day, Debra Brenegan, and Margo Barnes. A warm thank you to Ann and Kevin McQuade for sharing their writing sanctuary. And finally, to our families, who endured the writing process from the sidelines and never stopped cheering us onward, our love and appreciation always.

THE HORSE LOVER

PART ONE

CHAPTER ONE

A Sexy Find

They were out there somewhere. I scanned the horizon through the pickup's bug-spattered windshield. To the right, sunlight reflected off a small stream trickling in and out of view down the mountainside and meandering near this stretch of back road. Maybe they had been here. I pulled off the gravel, dragging a plume of dust, set the parking brake, and grabbed my binoculars from the front passenger seat. Hot wind whistled past me and bumped against the brown hills. I scouted for tracks in the soft, wet soil next to the stream. Not finding a one, I dredged up more patience and focused the binoculars on a distant ridge. This was the fifth time I had gone through this exercise since leaving Reno at sunrise. Sooner or later, I'd find them.

I panned the ridge. Left to right, right to left across clumps of scrub cedar and outcroppings of rock. I was about to turn back when the slightest of movements caught my attention. There, at the top of the ridge, was what I had driven miles to see. I held my breath to keep the binoculars steady against the rush of adrenaline.

A herd of horses began to gather, first two, then three, four, eight, ten, possibly fifteen. The slant of the sun shadowed their colors. One of the horses stood apart from the others, presumably the lead stallion. I had a sense he was looking directly at me, sizing me up, deciding if I was friend or foe.

"Come on, big boy, come on down," I said. "There's plenty of water. Take a good long drink."

The stallion turned his head as if listening. He looked at the herd for a moment, then took off at a gallop down the hill toward me, his family in tow. As the land leveled, he slowed and the other horses followed suit. They bowed their heads and began to graze on the scant clusters of grass. The stallion remained off to one side, ears alert and pointed, tail and mane blowing in the brisk breeze. Even though they were still half a mile away, I could count them now. Ten mares, four babies, and the stallion. All mustangs, all wild. Most were chestnut brown or black with black manes and tails. Two had solid golden coloring. The babies were light dusty brown, still too young to have grown into their colors. The smallest suckled on its mama, a thin sorrel mare with a large head. The stallion was jet black.

I watched, sometimes tucking the binoculars under my chin to give my arms a rest, though never moving more than a few slow inches at a time. I never had observed wild horses in their natural environment, yet I knew they were shy and skittish. They continued grazing their way down the last gentle slope of land toward the gurgling water. When they reached it, I felt like I had been awarded a gold medal for crossing the finish line of a strenuous race. I stood a quarter mile downstream from them. I wanted to hoot and holler in celebration but barely dared to breathe. Each horse took a long drink and splashed in the stream.

I remained still for who knows how long, twenty, thirty minutes, sweating under the Nevada summer sun. Finally I reached into the truck for a bottle of water. The movement triggered the stallion to give some sort of secret signal to the herd. Heads raised and whinnies floated in the air. The stallion took off running. Without hesitation, the horses turned in unison and gracefully followed him over a small hill. When I next spotted them, they were trotting over the ridge where they first had appeared. I focused the binoculars and saw the stallion stop on the crest of the ridge as if surveying whatever mysteries lay on the other side. His tail waved at me. In a blink, he disappeared from sight.

I stood in the cedar- and grass-scented wind, stood beneath the bowl of blue sky, no human or other vehicle in sight. A few hawks circled *overhead. I wondered what the stallion had thought of my presence. I only knew what I thought of his.*

I climbed in my truck and turned the key. The dream of two thousand wild mustangs running through long, thick prairie grass played across my mind. I turned toward Reno. The last thing in the truck's wake of dust was a whoop that soared as high as the hawks.

Without the South Dakota ranch, the wild horses and I would never have gotten to know each other. That much is certain. The ranch found me in the early summer of 1988, before a single wild horse stepped into my peripheral vision. At the time, I owned and managed two ranches and needed a third one about as much as I needed a permanent migraine. That's what I told Joe Nutter every time he pestered me to go see the old Arnold Ranch.

"But Alan," Joe would say, "I know how important good land is to you and, by gosh, this is thirty-five thousand acres of mouth-watering prairie." He was the consummate real estate agent. "It's beautiful. Absolutely incredible. And has the potential to be so productive. You of all people could turn this place around."

Every call. Beautiful. Incredible. Productive.

Joe wore me down like heels on a pair of cowboy boots. Finally, I said, "Goddamnit, Joe. I'll go with you just to get you off my back."

A few days later, I met him in the hamlet of Nenzel, Nebraska, population eighteen, and climbed in his pickup a bundle of grumbles. I hadn't taken my first sip of Joe's offered coffee when he turned off Highway 20 and headed north up a narrow dirt road.

"It's five miles to the state line and another five to headquarters," said Joe. He swung the wheel to skirt a pothole on the verge of becoming a crater. I quickly gave up drinking the coffee and concentrated on preventing my head from banging against the window. Joe pointed out a gnarled post, long divorced from a fence. "Welcome to South Dakota," he announced. Three potholes later, we clacked over a cattle guard. "Here we are, on the ranch." He looked at me for a reaction.

I couldn't reply, much less move. I had been slammed with an acute case of déjà vu. Somehow I knew this godforsaken road, knew it swerved right before we swerved right, knew what lay around each bend before we made the turn. This was more than a fleeting feeling. It intensified with every bump. I looked out over rolling, grass-covered hills that felt like old friends ready to embrace me, pour me a drink, and sit me down to reminisce about the good old days and the adventures we shared. I saw familiar fence lines, smelled the sweetness of familiar meadows. Without looking at the car's mileage, I knew we were nearing headquarters.

"Did you say there's a creek on one side of the main house?" I asked.

"No, I didn't say that," said Joe, "but there is." He gave me a quizzical side glance. "Have you been here before?"

"Not that I recall." I turned toward the window, unnerved. Not being prone to these types of experiences, I figured any explanation would sound as woo-woo as it felt.

We drove over a culvert and crested a hill. A cluster of buildings and corrals spread out before us. At the center stood a boxy three-story colonial home, white with dark green shutters and shaded by thick elms. A faded red barn anchored one end of the compound. When the ranch was at its zenith, this immense structure would have been its nerve center. The road forked in front of the house and Joe turned left, drove another hundred yards, pulled into an open graveled area, and parked near a pickup and two tractors. I stepped into air alive with the scent of freshly cut grass and livestock.

"The corrals are over there," said Joe, pointing past the tractors. "I believe there's a big roping arena and four or five smaller corrals. We'll check them out, but first let's see if the Pitkins are home."

We walked across an expanse of trim lawn. A tire swing hung

from one of the elms and I gave it a friendly push. Joe knocked on the door. I swished the blades of grass back and forth with my boot and tuned in to the midday conversations of redwing blackbirds and meadowlarks. A sense of belonging washed over me, dissolving weights on my shoulders. I wanted to run and touch everything like a small child returning home from a long vacation. I couldn't think beyond the moment; this was the only place in the world I needed to be.

"They must be gone," he said. "Too bad. I was hoping you could meet John and Debbie. Wonderful people. John knows every inch of this place. He's been managing it since Don Raymond fell in the bottle."

"I'm sure we'll meet at some point," I said, running my hand over paint peeling from the clapboards. I backed up from the house, craned my neck, and examined what I could see of the chimney and roof. The tuck-pointing looked intact, though some of the shingles lay crooked.

Joe mimicked my view. "Big old house, huh? Nine bedrooms."

"How old is it?"

"I think it dates back to the 1930s. Arnold and his wife had nine kids. Needed them to work the hundred thousand acres he owned back then. No wonder he became a local legend. After he died, the kids ended up selling off parcels of the land. Apparently none of them were big enough to fill his big shoes. Don Raymond bought thirty-five thousand acres."

We walked to the back of the house. A guesthouse sat a stone's throw away and just beyond was a doublewide trailer where Joe said Raymond lived until he filed for bankruptcy. What a shame he became an alcoholic. Having to sell this place must have added to whatever misery festered inside him. I would be heartbroken to lose such a treasure. The ranch charmed me, flirted with me as seductively as a starlet flirts with her fans. But I didn't need to

1. The main house and guesthouse at ranch headquarters

fall in love with it, because in some strange, inexplicable way, I already loved this ranch and had loved it forever.

We crossed the road near the trailer. A spring-fed creek pooled into a pond ringed with cattails and marsh grass. The water reflected the blue-and-white patchwork sky. A beaver had built a lodge on the far side and beyond its dwelling, a sea of prairie grass stretched out to a distant rise of hills. Its undulating surface mesmerized me and spoke of the land's great potential.

"Let's check out the rest of the place," said Joe. I forced myself to turn and follow. We crunched down the road back to the main house then veered off toward a bunkhouse and a shop. Both looked weathered around the eaves, windows, and doorframes. The glass in one of the bunkhouse windows had cracked. On the other side of the buildings were the corrals. The roping arena had to be a good five hundred feet long. A corner gate opened into a series of smaller corrals. In the farthest, a black horse and a bay grazed on hay. They raised their heads and looked at us curiously but were too intent on eating to walk over to say hello. Some of the corral posts looked worn and the rub boards that protected livestock were almost nonexistent. The neglect didn't deter me. Quite the opposite. I couldn't stop thinking about ways to refurbish the headquarters.

We slid open the gate of the arena and walked a few yards to the entrance of the barn. What a majestic building. One of the first things I would do is restore its proud red. A flash of reality intercepted my vision. How was I going to buy this ranch and what in God's name would I do with it besides fix it up?

"How you doing?" Joe asked. He looked at me oddly.

"Fine, just fine," I said, stepping into the dim light of the barn and readjusting my poker face. Joe led the way down the row of twenty horse stalls, then climbed a ladder into an empty, dormant hay loft.

"Pitkin said they baled about three thousand acres of hay in the meadow last summer," Joe said. In times past, this space would have been filled with loose hay, food for the workhorses.

Back outside, the sunlight glared bright. Joe suggested we drive over to the meadow on the south side of the ranch. The road went over Spring Creek and passed the pond. Joe slowed to allow a flock of wild turkeys to march across the gravel in front of us. A little farther on, the road turned left near a metal Quonset building.

"Don Raymond told me once that twenty vehicles could fit in there." I mumbled that he probably was right. The building, however, seemed insignificant compared to the scene in front of me. Joe stopped the truck at the edge of the sea of grass that extended beyond the pond. I got out and walked in a few yards. The grass was so thick I barely could see my shoes. For any grazing animal or rancher, this was the gold coast.

"The meadow extends around the back of those hills," Joe said, "and to the east. Then there's about another twelve hundred acres to the north." He dangled the carrot. "Do you want to go look over there? Or drive over to the Little White River? It snakes around for a good five miles through the ranch and is real pretty."

"That's okay," I said. "I've seen enough for today." I didn't add that it wasn't necessary because on some level I knew those meadows and places and indeed, they were perfect, beautiful and fit for ownership. Maybe Joe was a good poker player and could read my face because he didn't look perturbed. We got back in the truck and bounced back toward Highway 20. We passed the flock of wild turkeys, maybe twelve or fourteen, bobbling along the road in single file, heading out on some secret journey. At the gnarled post, Joe popped the question. "So what do you think?"

"Well, I gotta be honest. My rule of thumb is not to tangle with property on the brink of foreclosing. But this is one gorgeous ranch. Not sure what I would use it for." But did it matter?

"You're a good cattle rancher," Joe said.

"I'm not so sure I want to invest in any more cattle. Right now I'm running a total of four thousand cows. That might be putting too much risk in one place."

"You'll think of something," said Joe.

We pulled into Nenzel and I promised to call him within two days.

I climbed in my pickup and swallowed some cold coffee, hoping it would restore my senses. I had my arms wrapped around the old Arnold Ranch in a big bear hug and I couldn't let go. But this overwhelming desire to own the ranch was totally illogical. It bucked the core principles that guided me in business. I knew that unprofitable, troubled ranches should be avoided like melting ice on a pond. My dad had ingrained that lesson in me before I even broke my first horse, and his dad had ingrained it in him.

Furthermore, it was a family mantra never to invest in unneeded property. I currently co-owned and managed two ranches: the Lazy B, a 198,000-acre chunk of high desert straddling southern Arizona and New Mexico, and the Rex Ranch, a 45,000-acre parcel of prairie nestled in the Sand Hills of Nebraska. My Cessna was getting worn out arcing between the Southwest and the Midwest. For certain, my life did not need this ranch. Plus, I only took calculated risks. Too many times I had seen cattle prices bounce like a rubber ball on asphalt, watched miserly rain clouds disperse drops that barely dented the sand, and felt the slap of governmental regulations that gummed up well-oiled ranching practices. Excessive risk is like a saddlebag stuffed with fool's gold; it weighs the horse down and doesn't pay off. So why gamble? Because I sensed that within the boundaries of the old Arnold Ranch lay something special. A journey? A destiny? A fate? My soul needed to know.

That night I made a series of phone calls. First, I gushed to my wife, Sue, who was back in Arizona. During my absences, she was my eyes and ears at Lazy B.

"I think that pen is already in your hand ready to sign an offer," she said. "I'm already looking forward to seeing the place when the time is right."

It was a green light, but I needed a different kind of green. I phoned each of my business partners. Beautiful, incredible, productive, I repeated over and over. My enthusiasm must have swayed them, because all five agreed to go deeper into debt. Forty-eight hours later, I made a conservative offer on the old Arnold Ranch. That beautiful, beat-up, bankrupt ranch. It was like rolling a little white marble counterclockwise in the groove of the spinning roulette wheel. I'm pretty certain my dad and granddad did flips in their graves that day and not from joy. The offer did not include the forty head of cattle running on the property, but it did include every machine and building, as well as the big house, home to the Pitkin family.

How was I going to staff the old Arnold Ranch? The question nudged me from a deep sleep one night. Less than a week had passed since Joe Nutter submitted my offer to the bank and already my mind was grappling with management issues. I would need to hire a foreman. I had a fabulous one on Lazy B and a cantankerous one on the Rex Ranch. Joe had spoken highly of John Pitkin. If he equaled his reputation, the job search might end before it began. Regardless, I owed this Pitkin fellow a visit since his future was in my hands and he was probably suffering a bit of anxiety wondering what was in store for him and his family. A call to the Pitkins would be the first order of business in the morning. I punched the pillow, rolled over, and tried to still my thoughts.

Two days later Debbie Pitkin and I sat on the south porch of the big house, glasses of ice tea sweating in our hands. She was telling me what grades her four kids were in when a screen door slammed at the back of the house.

"Here comes John," said Debbie.

Heavy footsteps echoed inside and a tall man wearing cowboy boots walked through the doorway. "John Pitkin," he said, extending a hand. He was a handsome man, dark haired, square jawed, with a smile that made him look about eighteen.

Debbie went to refill our glasses, leaving John and me to chat about seasonal rain levels and temperatures and how the hay was growing in the meadows. He asked what it was like in Arizona this time of year. I described the dry, hot climate and the scant grass that poked up through the desert pastures.

"Not sure I could handle days over a hundred," he said. "Guess I'm acclimated to this country."

"How long have you lived on the ranch?" I said.

"We moved here about six years ago. I was working for Don Raymond at the time, down near North Platte. Debbie and I both grew up in the Platte River Valley. Don owned a small feedlot and I started working for him when I was a teenager. Over time, I had a chance to wear all sorts of hats—mechanic, farmer, cowboy, vet, truck driver."

"Which did you like best?"

"Oh, I always preferred working with the cattle and horses. That's why I wanted to tag along when Raymond bought this ranch. He planned to run a thousand head on it, and I thought it would be a good way to learn more about ranching. First time I came up here, I fell in love with the place. Don has four daughters and I'm the closest thing he has to a son, so I didn't have to twist his arm to let me join him. We had a couple of good years at the start, but then the drinking got the best of him. The last few years haven't been too much fun. He sold several bunches of cattle at the bar when he was too drunk to make a good deal. I've spent more time keeping creditors at bay than I have ranching." John and Debbie exchanged a commiserating look.

"I can teach you good ranching practices," I said. John leaned forward like he was ready for class to begin right now. "I've always been a hands-on rancher and that's what I intend to keep doing. I'm not coming in here as a mere investor. Though I do need someone to teach me in return." John looked a bit surprised. "Having done most of my ranching in Arizona, I'm not expert on what grasses are native to this ranch or how to handle livestock during a blizzard. I spent only one winter on the Rex Ranch and it was mild." John nodded in understanding.

We continued talking for well over an hour. John had an aura that commanded attention and openly shared his frustrations and accomplishments. It didn't seem to bother him that I didn't have a specific game plan for the ranch. As long as he could work the land and the livestock, he would be happy.

The ice tea had long disappeared when I decided it was time to take my leave. "It's been a real treat to sit here and talk to both of you. I have a pretty strong feeling that my offer will be accepted and I'll become the owner of this place. At least I hope so. I'd like you to stay on as foreman if you're interested, John. We can work out the details, but I promise you two things. I won't fall in the bottle and your family can continue living in this house."

I could almost hear John and Debbie's joint sigh of relief.

"That's the best plan I've heard in some time," said John, and we shook on a future together.

With the property in escrow and the Pitkin family in place, I faced the facts that now stood staring me down. Talk about a holy shit moment. I had persuaded the bank to lend me money to buy the ranch, which meant I had two monthly mortgages but only one ranch, the Rex Ranch, generating income; Lazy B belonged to my family and its profits were off-limits. I found myself waking up in the middle of the night lost in an arithmetic jungle, counting the number of calves I needed to sell in order to cover those mortgages. I felt uneasy about running cattle on a third ranch lest the market nosedive and no profits cross the finish line for anyone. Finally, weary from sleep deprivation, I shifted my anxious mind into creative mode and tried to think of a different way to generate income on the new ranch. That's when the roulette wheel came to a stop and the little white marble dropped to its destiny.

CHAPTER TWO

Opportunity Walks In

"If you move your cattle between pastures regularly—and that might be every two to three weeks or even two to three days depending on your system—you'll be able to run more cattle because you have more grass. This is one of the tremendous advantages of timed grazing. And it works with animals of all kinds—goats, sheep, even horses." I paused to gauge the reaction of the hundred people in front of me. Eyebrows scrunched. "I know it may sound strange to move your cattle so often," I said, noticing a giant of a man slip into the back of the conference room. "But this grazing system works."

The stranger started waving at me, then mouthing something like "I need to talk to you." For a moment I lost my concentration. I pointed at him and nodded my head. Members of the New Mexico Cattle Growers' Association turned in their seats to look at the distraction. Despite the cowboy hat, anyone could see that this fellow, dressed as he was in a Pendleton shirt and khakis, was no southwestern rancher. I took a sip of water and attempted to step back in stride with my keynote address.

After the questions and the blue-jeaned crowd thinned, I was left standing face to face with the stranger who had demanded my attention. He looked to be about six -foot four and at least ten years older than I, with a craggy face that bespoke years spent in sun, wind, and adventure.

"Alan Day, I'm Dayton Hyde," he said. A slight western drawl draped across his words. "But my friends call me Hawk."

So this was Dayton Hyde. He had a reputation within the ranching community as an enthusiastic not-quite-born-in-the-saddle cowboy, a fellow horse lover, an outdoorsman, a talented writer, and a dreamer.

"Pleased to meet you, Dayton. I've heard your name bantered around these parts." Our hands met in a firm grip. "I appreciate you waiting. Looked like you had something on your mind."

"Well, sir, I do. I'm mighty glad to catch up with you." He leaned in closer and lowered his voice a notch. "There's a real important issue that I want to discuss with you. Thought after all that talking up there you might need a drink. Can I buy you one?"

He clapped my shoulder like we had already agreed, but in such a friendly way and with such a big old grin that I could hardly say no.

We headed toward the hotel bar and took up residence at a quiet corner table. A waitress appeared to take our orders of scotch and water.

Dayton briefly filled me in on the ranch he owned in Oregon where his wife, Gerta, his son, and his pet wolf resided. Seriously, I said, a pet wolf? He laughed and explained that when things got a little prickly in the house his wolf never picked on him. He had spent the better part of the last fifteen years building a big dam on his ranch and creating what he claimed was the best trout stream in North America, but now he was spending more time on a new ranch in South Dakota, a hilly, five-thousand-acre slice of heaven. I was just going to tell him about the offer I had made a month ago on the Arnold Ranch when the waitress returned. Ice chinked against glass as she set drinks and napkins on the table.

Dayton shifted in his chair and extended a pair of long legs. Before I could utter a word, he said, "So, my friend, how familiar are you with the wild horse fiasco in this country?"

His question caught me off guard. As a rancher, horses had

been part of my life forever but I had never taken much interest in government-owned wild horses. "I know there's controversy," I said, trying to recall what I had read recently. "I'm thinking it's similar to the stir we had in Arizona over the wild burros. The Bureau of Land Management determined there were too many inhabiting the Grand Canyon and went and hauled them out on slings beneath helicopters."

Dayton nodded. "Heard about that. Hope it didn't frighten those poor devils to death." A hint of a frown dipped his mouth.

"As I understand the wild horse situation," I said, "everyone is pretty pissed off. The ranchers. The BLM. The wild horse lovers. But I admit to being a bit removed from the details."

"You're right, it extends further," said Dayton. A little mountain peaked between his eyebrows. "Let me give you the down and dirty."

Roughly forty thousand wild mustangs roamed and grazed federal lands, too many for the square miles assigned to them. To prevent entire herds from starving, the BLM rounded up horses in a given area and moved them to holding facilities. Cowboys on horseback and in helicopters descended on unsuspecting mustangs. Sometimes the deafening choppers chased the horses for miles down canyons and over hills. Older horses might be injured while frantically trying to escape. Mothers became separated from babies, families torn apart. Once gathered in makeshift corrals, the horses were shipped to facilities around the country. The main sorting facility was located at Palomino Valley in Nevada.

Dayton's cloud of disgust hovered over us. I didn't like to hear stories about cruelty to horses, any horses, and I could feel the seeds of discomfort begin to sprout.

"Once captured," he continued, "the mustangs get sorted. Adoptables, including colts and fillies, go one way; unadoptables, including most of the mothers, go another. Some get turned back on the range. As you can imagine, the adoptables are pretty as the pictures in a coffee-table book. Sleek, trim, shiny haired. I've seen palominos, red roans, black, brown, you name it. Gorgeous creatures. The most desired of all are the Pryors."

I knew horse people who drooled over the mustangs gathered in the Pryor Mountains of Montana, animals descended directly from horses ridden by the Spanish conquistadors. They are some of the finest, strongest, most regal horses. Most often they are duns, lighter brown, with a stripe running down the back, a dorsal stripe on their shoulder, and distinctive leg stripes. If you get one, it's kind of like finding a '57 Thunderbird that's never been driven.

"But not every wild horse is adoptable. There's the crippled. The one-eyed. The thin. The shaggy. The old." He ticked off each description on a finger. "Who wants those horses? Nobody. So the government's stuck with them. And do they know what to do? Hell, no!" Dayton sliced his hand through the air. "Those horses are warehoused in holding pens where 'long-term' turns out to be forever. A lifelong horse prison."

I knew the BLM gathered horses, though I didn't know the details of how, and even knew a couple of people who had adopted a wild mustang. But I had never wondered what happened to the extras. The unadoptables. The unloved.

"They're bored, Alan. So bored they eat each other's manes and tails. Yeah, that's the same look I had. Didn't believe it. So I took a little road trip down to the facility in Mule Shoe, Texas, and I'll be damned, those animals—the revered icons of the West," he added with a fist bang on the table, "were stuck in corrals. It's one big bureaucratic mess where the solution doesn't fit the problem. What's more, it's costing the government $2.65 per head per day to fund this stupidity. Hell, these beautiful animals aren't meant to live in jail. They're meant to run on the open prairie, run with the wind whipping through their manes." His arms spread open like the wings of a large bird. "Sure, they need grass to live on, and grass might be scant, but you know what else they need?" He shifted his legs under his chair and leaned his elbows on the table. "Freedom. They need freedom."

I felt like I was listening to a John Wayne soliloquy, perched on the edge of my seat, too engrossed to eat the popcorn the waitress had set in the middle of the table. I asked if they were abused, and he waffled. The horses weren't starved. They had good flesh and nice coats, but they weren't happy.

"Imagine a hundred professional athletes," he said, "crowded into a building with no rooms big enough to exercise in. To add to their misery, you tell them they can never get out and run again, they are destined to live in this one cinder block building. No matter what you feed those athletes, they remain downtrodden, frustrated, angry people. Wild horses are born to run across miles of open land, just like athletes. That's what they do. Over the prairie, across the hills, through canyons, they can track miles and miles each day. So even though they're being fed and physically cared for, prohibiting them from doing what nature intended could be considered abuse."

Wild horses couldn't be slaughtered, that much I knew. Wild Horse Annie had seen to that. Velma B. Johnston made national news for almost two decades starting in the 1950s after driving behind a truck loaded with captured mustangs. She noticed blood dripping onto the highway. Careful not to be seen, she followed the truck to a rendering plant where she watched men unload the horses. A yearling fell and was trampled to death by the other frightened mustangs. The event incited her to launch a grassroots campaign to get Congress to pass legislation protecting the wild horses, which it finally did in the early seventies.

"So what do you propose to do?" I asked.

He swirled his glass as if watching words melt off the ice. In a somber tone he said, "It's my goal to take these unwanted, unloved horses and put them on good range where they can roam again. Roam and be cared for. Not live in those goddamn foolish feedlots.

And we can do it for less than half the cost the government now pays the feedlots."

Interesting idea, but how did any of this pertain to me? Come on, wild horses? I was a cattle rancher. Yes, I loved my horses. Alongside the soil flowing in my blood was a river of love for my horses. They had been a part of my extended family as much as the cowboys who helped raise me and spent their lifetime on Lazy B. Chico, Little Joe, Saber, Aunt Jemima, Blackberry, Little Charlie Brown, and so many others. We had shared cowboying adventures of the unbelievable kind. But my connection to herds of wild horses? Nil.

"Here's what I propose." Dayton held his hands up as if framing the idea. "I want to establish a wild horse sanctuary. It's never been done before but I've given it a lot of thought and I believe if it's set up correctly, it could work. We need the government's approval and support, of course. And we need land."

At that moment the scotch, or maybe something on a grander scale, shifted my brain into a new gear. A panoramic vision of the lush prairie grass on the South Dakota ranch spread across my mind's eye. I had been hoping to find a use for the land other than running cattle. Might it be suitable range for a herd of mustangs?

"How many unadoptables are we talking about in the holding pens?"

"Almost two thousand," Dayton replied.

I just about had to scoop my jaw off the table. Trying to envision that many horses on the ranch was a ballbuster. I'd run more head of cattle than that before, but horses? I had no clue how much fifty horses ate, much less two thousand. Or what their grazing patterns would be. I wouldn't bet my next drink on the number that could thrive on the South Dakota ranch. The thought of managing a ranch full of two-thousand-pound animals that have had minimal experience with humans, and that mostly negative, evoked more than a little trepidation. It was like going from being a pilot of a little Cessna to a pilot of a 747 jetliner without lessons.

Yet, if I took a deep breath and dove below the fear, something felt possible here. Perhaps the government's coffers could support such a venture. Perhaps the land could too. Good luck had stuffed itself in my pocket long ago, and adventure had been my friend since I was old enough to scramble on the back of Chico and head out on the range, trying my five-year-old darnedest to keep up with the big cowboys. Usually I was contemplating adventures that involved animals I knew — ranch horses, cattle. But with this I could very well be stepping in over my Stetson.

Dayton continued. "The idea of a wild horse sanctuary has never occurred to the BLM, or if it has they haven't gotten around to trying it. Most likely they need persuading that it's a sensible, solid game plan to contract with and pay a private landowner to care for two thousand animals nobody wants."

I had been working with the tightfisted BLM all my professional life. They would need persuading all right, bales of it.

"The reason that I contacted you, Alan, is because you have an in with the BLM folks. All your ranching buddies tell me that the BLM thinks you walk on water."

I shook my head. "Not sure that I'd go that far. They don't exactly send me birthday cards."

"Okay, well, let's just say you can hook and catch their attention and reel them in. They don't know me from the next wrangler and would brush me off faster than a biting fly."

Dayton was right on one thing. The BLM and I had a good rapport. When they needed rancher input on land and grazing issues, they often asked me to participate on boards and panels. They had designated me a steward of the land for my work in grass management on Lazy B. Most crusty cowboys considered the BLM their enemy. But that attitude only made their lives miserable. I chose not to walk down that road. Over time, I inadvertently became the point man for other ranchers. I would relay their issues to the BLM, go to bat for those boys, and try to hollow out common ground that allowed bureaucrats to be bureaucrats and ranchers to be ranchers. We didn't always agree, sometimes we were miles apart on our stances, but other times we could carve out a compromise acceptable to both sides. And if we didn't agree, we'd keep talking.

I took a sip of scotch and tried to visualize the South Dakota ranch with horses on it. For a moment, I saw myself sitting on Aunt Jemima. We stood on the top of a hill, the prairie below sloping down toward the Little White River. Horses young and old, a spectrum of browns, blacks, and whites, grazed before us. Healthy, thick grass beckoned. Something inside of me was waking up, warming to the idea. A little voice said the mustangs would thrive on that windswept prairie.

But then another vision hightailed it in. The horses shivered in a blizzard. Could we shelter them from the killing wind? Would we have enough hay and could we get it to them, or would they have to slip across ice, paw through snow, and graze the dead grass? Would older horses survive winter's grip? The ranch was tuned to caring for cattle during tough winters, but horses might tow a different set of challenges.

I flitted back to the possible stream of income in this wacky idea. The Bureau of Land Management had a budget in place to pay for the care of horses. We needed that first and foremost since neither Dayton nor I was in a position to give away services. Maybe we could charge a lower rate and save the government money. Could this be an industry waiting to happen? Perhaps. If nothing else, it seemed to be an opportunity to do something gigantic, something that had never been done before.

"You know, Hawk, this is a pretty interesting proposal. I might very well be able to open the door with the BLM. I can talk to Les Rosencrantz, the state director of Arizona, and I've met the national director, Bob Burford, a pretty nice guy. A rancher from Grand

Junction, Colorado. I bet we could get an audience with him if we needed to. But there's an even more interesting thing about your timing." I leaned forward and spun the basket of popcorn. Dayton looked at me, curious.

"As it happens I'm in the process of buying a thirty-five-thousand-acre ranch in the Sand Hills of southern South Dakota."

Stress lines evaporated from his face, and his body came to attention.

"Think a couple thousand mustangs might be able to live up there?" I asked.

I could almost see his mind holding up this piece of the puzzle, the last of the border pieces, recognizing it, and pushing it into place. The only sound that escaped his mouth was a whispered "goddamn." After a moment of sitting stock still, he let loose a throw-your-head-back yelp that would summon any pack of coyotes. Cowboy hats swiveled. Seeing two faces plastered with three parts excitement and a shot of disbelief, they turned back to their conversations.

Then in true cowboy fashion, Dayton "Hawk" Hyde said, "Let's order another drink and chew on this one for a while."

Man, was I jacked on the drive from Las Cruces back to Lazy B, and not from the scotch. I had been a cattle rancher for so long that entertaining an idea not involving cattle felt exhilarating, foreign, and daring all at the same time. Not even in my wildest, far-out imaginings could I have thought up a wild horse sanctuary. But here it was, served to me on a silver platter. The miles zipped by as my mind shifted the pieces of this puzzle to see how they might fit together. Dayton had the vision. The BLM had the money. I had the ranching experience and business skills. The land offered space and grass. Then there were the horses, possibly two thousand of them.

The idea of working with horses felt as natural as the idea of working with cattle. After all, horses were as much a part of my life as my parents, my sisters, the Lazy B cowboys, the land. The benchmarks of my childhood and adolescence involved horses. The first time I mounted a horse without help. The first time I brought a runaway cow back to the herd without help. The first time I roped a calf and didn't lose my rope. The first time I rode a bucking horse and didn't get thrown.

My first horse was a little wild mustang named Chico. He had been part of a herd of twenty or thirty that ranged the flanks of Steeple Rock Mountain, just north of Lazy B. A local cowboy decided to capture and break some of the horses, but the fleet-footed animals proved too elusive and quick for him, so he decided to try to shoot one. The mustangers of that era would aim their gun at a specific spot on the horse's neck. If they hit their target, they could stun and knock down the animal without killing him. Before the horse could recover his senses, they would throw a halter on him. It was a brutal way to capture mustangs and one that Congress eventually outlawed. Chico always had a scar on the top of his neck where the bullet creased him.

Chico became my best friend almost as soon as I could walk. A pretty bay color with a star on his forehead, he was a small horse, too small for a cowboy, but just right for a child. Chico and I lived many adventures together while he stood patiently in the corral and let me clamber over him like a jungle gym. One day I would be the cowboy chasing and catching wild cattle to the amazement of the other cowboys. The next day I was an Indian stalking game and evading the cavalry. The fact that Chico came from a wild horse herd enamored me. When I was old enough to ride, Chico would go at a speed I was capable of handling and no faster. When I fell off and cried and grew angry with him, he would stand still and patiently wait for me to collect myself and get back on. He took care of me more hours than my mother did and at least as well.

Chico and I were a team the day I became a real cowboy. World War II left my dad short of help, so he allowed me to join the roundup at Old Camp on the southern part of Lazy B. It was to be a long, hard day, just the kind of day for a five-year-old to make a hand. I don't remember breakfast at 3:00 a.m. or the long bumpy ride in the pickup out to Robb's Well where the horses awaited us, but I do recall the sweet, acrid smell of the horses, the squeak and creak of the leather saddles as the cowboys tossed them on the animals' backs, the snorting and farting of the horses as the cowboys mounted. Because I wasn't tall enough to get my foot in the stirrup, I had to lead Chico to the water trough to mount.

We all set out, Chico and I riding side by side with the cowboys. Many times, I had heard them make fun of dudes, the wannabes who could never get cowboying quite right. I was determined not to be a dude, and this was the day to show I wasn't one. After riding a couple of miles, the cowboys split into groups to search for cows in different parts of the range. The plan was for everyone to arrive at Old Camp by noon, cattle in front. I split off with Jim Brister and another cowboy, Ira, and started the cows heading down a wide canyon. After a bit, Jim instructed me to keep the herd moving, that he and Ira were going to work Lightning Canyon and push the cattle into Rock Tank Canyon, which connected with this main canyon a mile down. They would catch up with me in about an hour.

What a big job! I sat straight in my saddle and beamed. Of course, a five-year-old has no idea how long an hour or how far a mile is. Nor does he realize that his mentors trusted the horse he rode to take care of him.

The cattle knew water awaited them at Old Camp, so keeping them going downhill proved easy work. I'm sure within fifteen minutes I thought an hour had passed, but I kept doing my job. Pretty soon, though, I started getting thirsty and I had to pee. I couldn't dismount because I needed help getting back in the saddle. I kept Chico and the cows going, determined not to be in the wrong place at the wrong time.

The cicadas started to buzz in the hot, dry air. They grew louder and louder until the whole world was buzzing. The buzzing crept into my head and strung itself between my ears. Certainly we had gone more than a mile and much longer than an hour. Thirst joined the buzzing. All I wanted was a drink of water and to pee. I wondered if this is what it was like to go crazy.

I started to cry. I bent over Chico's soft neck and let tears drip onto his hide. "Chico, where's Jim and Ira? They must have gone off and left us." My chance to be a real cowboy was crashing in on me. I was in danger of becoming a dude. And on my first roundup. I needed to cowboy-up before someone saw me crying.

Chico didn't seem too perturbed that we had been walking the canyon by ourselves forever. He meandered at the same pace, occasionally nudging the back end of a cow that had slowed. This helped calm me. I had wiped the tears from my face and was contemplating how to pee from the saddle when I heard cows bawl from a side canyon. A cowboy's yell followed. We were saved!

Jim and Ira arrived a few minutes later. I'm sure they saw tear streaks on my dusty cheeks but neither said a word. And of course, Chico never let on that there had been a problem since by his standards we had done just fine.

After lunch, the cowboys branded and sorted the cattle, and then we drove them back to Robb's Well. By the end of the fifteen-hour day, I was one exhausted, proud little cowboy. No one could call me a dude. I had made a hand.

I turned off the state highway onto Lazy B's eight-mile ranch road that started in New Mexico and ended in Arizona. Somehow being on Lazy B made me feel that much closer to Chico. He and I had ridden over these hills and dales; he had grazed in the horse pasture through which this road curved. Even though by age twelve I had outgrown riding Chico, I never outgrew my love for him. He had taught me so many lessons, including patience and how to keep the faith.

I pulled into headquarters and parked. The new moon thickened the darkness so I could barely see the outline of horses fifty yards away in the corral. My boots ground the gravel. One of the horses snorted; another answered with a low nicker. Maybe they were reading my mind and the question simmering there. Would my love affair with horses begin with one wild horse and end with a herd of them? The moon would cycle through its phases almost fifty times before shedding light on the answer.

CHAPTER THREE

The Dream Takes Shape

"I'm getting dizzy watching you pace in there," said Sue. She was in the family room adjacent to my office. "This house can't contain your excitement. We need to get out of here." Her tone indicated there would be no arguing. "Why don't you go throw the old mattress in the pickup and cut some steaks from that quarter of beef hanging in the cooler. I'll pack some potatoes and wine and we can head up to Horseshoe Canyon."

So the day after my conversation with Dayton, still afloat in a bubble of possibilities, my wife and I drove an hour across the flatlands of Lazy B to the part known as the Gruwell Ranch, then up fifteen hundred feet into a juniper-filled canyon where the ruts of the pickup trail ended in a flat, shaded area. With the nearest human at least ten miles away, this was my haven for chewing on a challenge, a dream, or a grilled steak.

We unloaded the cooler and dinner provisions and spread charcoal in the grill. I opened a bottle of wine and grabbed two glasses. "Let's walk up there before we start the fire," I said, pointing the bottle at a two-foot-high rock wall about a hundred yards above us.

We climbed through the mellowing light and leaned our backs against the warm stones. The wine gurgled into a glass. I handed it to Sue, then poured my own.

"Did I ever tell you this was the site of the Stein's Pass Indian skirmish?"

"At least ten times," she said, poking her elbow into my side.

I liked to come up here and imagine how the battle between the Apache Indians and the Seventh U.S. Cavalry might have been fought. Starting from Stein's Pass ten miles east, the cavalry had driven the Indians to this spot, where they forced the band of Apaches higher and higher. The Indians had climbed this hill on foot and erected this rock battlement to shield them from the soldiers' bullets. The cavalry, not wanting to storm the fortress at dusk, decided to hole up in the canyon's bottom until morning. Shortly after sunrise, they discovered the Apaches had disappeared. In the dead of night, the fierce, small band had fled by foot over the mountains, running for miles without leaving a trace. I hoped the toughness, grit, and patience of those natives would transfer to me.

"Here's to figuring out if we can make this sanctuary work," I said. Our glasses pinged. The red liquid held the rays of sun. Its sliding warmth matched that of the stones. "Tell me what you're thinking, sweetheart."

Sue savored a sip before answering. "I'm thinking this proposition has hit some chord in you. I can hear it resonating. And if I know you like I do, you're not going to turn your back. You're going to throw your saddle right over this baby and run with it as far as you can. So someway, somehow, we are going to make this wild horse thing work. In fact, we're not leaving this mountain until we figure it out. Otherwise we could be headed for a case of regrets, and who needs that?" She took my hand in hers.

Through the rest of the wine and into dinner, we carefully laid a foundation under Dayton's grandiose plan. I racked my brain to identify all the parts we had to play to make the sanctuary a success. First, I would have to spend extended periods of time in South Dakota learning the ranch inside and out. This would leave Sue with a larger role in Lazy B's day-to-day operations. She would need to work closely with our foreman, Greg Webb, and relay details to me every day by phone. She already was an angel caregiver to my aging mother and even more of that responsibility would fall on her shoulders. For my part, I needed to discuss this venture with my partner in the Rex Ranch, Alan Stratman. My guess was that he would want to focus his efforts entirely in Nebraska. I would continue to be involved in decisions there as we moved forward to meet our business goals, but I felt comfortable turning the reins over to him. I also needed to give John Pitkin the heads-up that the plan was to fill the old Arnold Ranch pastures with horses, not cattle. I didn't foresee an issue there. Dayton and I would lobby the BLM, and somewhere along the way, I would get educated about wild horses. How exactly did one go about handling a couple thousand renegade mustangs?

As the campfire reflected off the dark walls of the canyon, Sue and I hashed out detail after detail, stacking them like the rocks in the battlement above us. Only a few embers glowed when we settled onto the lumpy mattress, a light blanket covering us. The choir of a million stars serenaded us with their sparkles. I pulled my wife close, felt her curves form into mine.

"We're partners in this one, baby. If something's not going right, you have to let me know," I whispered in her ear.

"I will. I promise," she said, wrapping her legs around me. It was our turn to serenade the stars.

I drifted into the depth of night feeling like I was on the brink of a long journey. The road stretched ahead of me like an Arizona highway, untouched by snow and ice and salt spreaders. Smooth blacktop. Bright yellow stripes. Even on freshly paved roads, blowouts occur. Here and there you see scraps of shredded tires on the shoulder of the road, sometimes in the middle, too. Hurdles that you don't discern until the last minute. One way or another, you get around them. Sometimes you swerve, sometimes you drive over them. I would need to keep a careful eye on this road and a steady hand on the wheel.

The minute Sue and I returned to ranch headquarters the next morning, I made a beeline to my office. If there was one person in the Bureau of Land Management who would be open to an innovative idea and who had climbed the bureaucratic ladder high enough to help, it was Les Rosencranz. Les and I had developed a friendly relationship during the years Lazy B had been under his jurisdiction. He was a good listener, a straight shooter, and a kindred lover of the land.

At 8:05 a.m., I picked up the phone.

"Hey, how are you Al? Haven't heard from you in quite a stretch. What's going on?" His upbeat voice held a smile. We caught up on our comings and goings.

I veered into business. "Les, I've got an idea that involves the BLM. You've heard me think out of the box before, but I'm so far out of the box I can hardly see it."

"Nothing like starting out the day with a little excitement, man. Lay it on me."

I felt like I was taking a running start and leaping over the Grand Canyon. "I'm thinking about starting a wild horse sanctuary," I said in a surreal airborne moment.

Silence, then what sounded like a coffee mug clunking against wood. "You're right, that's one I never heard before," Les said. "But it's a hell of an issue for us."

Thump. I had hit dirt. Whether it was pay dirt or burial dirt, I had no clue.

Les listened to my broad-brush narrative of how a privately operated, federally subsidized wild horse sanctuary could benefit government coffers, overgrazed land, and a couple thousand unadoptable mustangs, a narrative I would soon be able to recite in my sleep.

"So have I lost it or not?" I asked.

"Well, I'm not ready to call it harebrained, but it definitely is unconventional. I do have one question for you, though," Les said.

"When those horses charge off to the next county, how are you going to get them turned back and bring 'em home?"

I had been thinking about this prickly issue since the sun roused me out of a sound sleep. Wild horses balk at following directions from a two-legged alien creature wearing a funny hat. You can train a mustang individually, but it would take years to put two thousand through private lessons. I didn't care what the government might pay, no way was I going to spend my days chasing horses around a ranch.

I said, "I'm not a hundred percent certain, but I may have a solution. It's based on a training program we used on Lazy B to gentle the wild cattle."

"*Gentle* wild cattle?" said Les. "Did I hear that right?"

Gentling the cattle had been one of the improvements I made on the ranch after my dad became less active in managing it. Unlike most ranchers, he had preferred to ranch on foot, so he kept horse riding to a minimum. During spring and fall roundups, the cowboys would drive a herd of cattle into the corral and he would have them off their horses faster than lightning hits the ground. They'd run their legs off opening and closing gates and getting the cattle settled. Of course the cowboys bitched. They wanted to be in the corrals on horseback. But I walked in different boots than my dad. I'd been raised around cowboys like Jim Brister, who practically lived on a horse, and like Jim, I loved working horseback. When I took over the ranch, roundups had more running than a tri-state track meet. Because our cattle weren't accustomed to seeing a man mounted on a horse, they had become increasingly ornery and wild, and they spooked when you rode up to them in the pasture. With pastures as big as eighty square miles, the herd had a fine time playing hide-and-seek with us.

My real wake-up call came one spring during roundup. The cowboys and I spent two hard days gathering heifers out of the Cottonwood pasture, where they had spent the past year maturing to adulthood. We finally got them in the corrals at headquarters, a temporary holding spot. The next day I instructed a handful of cowboys to drive half the herd up into the Black Hills, where they would join a larger herd. I should have appointed one of the hands to take up the lead and set the pace, but I didn't. The cowboys all hung out at the back of the bunch. They told me later that when the group started the two-thousand-foot climb up the rocky canyon, the heifers charged so fast that the cowboys couldn't catch them to slow them down. Three cows ran themselves to death and died right in the middle of the canyon. I was horrified. I was not going to be a rancher who killed cows by running them to death. I resolved to make major changes in our handling of the cattle.

But how could we get the cattle to change their perception of us? One way was to invest in more cowboys and faster horses. But that would continue to promote unwanted commotion and distress among the animals. Another way was to bait the cattle with feed, a common practice among ranchers. During the year the heifers lived in the pasture growing from six-month-old calves to eighteen-month-old cows, we could go out with a truck, honk the horn, and spread a trail of corn or hay. Over time, the cattle would recognize the sound of the blaring horn, associate it with food, and not get all jittery. But that didn't address the imminent problem. Cowboys on horseback would still incite panic, and off we would be to the races.

I decided the next time we weaned calves, we would put them through an intensive gentling program while they were still in the headquarters corrals. Get them to recognize us. The cowboys thought my marbles had bounced on the ground and gotten buried in the dust. But the boys wanted their paychecks. So after we weaned that next group of calves, three cowboys and I saddled up, went into the corral, and talked to those babies. Real calm, real friendly.

We held the group of 150 in a corral corner, then started driving them down the side. Of course they broke and ran all over the place, so we gathered them again, all the while chatting like we were best friends. Every time we tried to drive them, they'd scatter. Twenty minutes later, the calves were pooped. We gave them a break but came back three more times that day and went through the same drill. After four or five days, the training started to stick. They began to follow a man on horse and a horse's butt. They no longer feared us. If a calf left the group, one of the cowboys would race after and run her hard, not harming her, just making her uncomfortable. The lesson learned? If you go off on your own, life is uncomfortable; if you stay with the herd, life is good. Pretty soon they'd follow the lead around the corral, then through the gate and out to an adjoining small pasture. It was an exercise in repetitive teaching, like teaching kindergarteners to stay in a line and file into the lunchroom. By the time we turned those cattle out for the year, they were the best-behaved bunch on the ranch.

I stopped pacing, plunked in my desk chair, and took a sip of cold coffee. "But we still didn't have proof the training worked," I said. Les grunted in acknowledgment. I stretched my feet up on the desk. A slice of sunshine hugged the tip of my boot. "During the next twelve months, we'd drive out in a pickup periodically to check on them, make sure the windmill was pumping water, restock their salt supply if necessary. So the time comes to gather them. I take a full crew out, not knowing what to expect because those heifers haven't seen us on horseback for a year. In the past, when we rode within a half mile, the cattle would look up and rev up their jets. But this time, we get to the half-mile mark, spread out ready for action, and those cows? They don't lift a head. A quarter mile, and all is calm. I'm about ready to fall off my horse. Now we're right around the herd and some of those heifers finally glance up as if to say, 'Oh, hello, it's you.' So I say right back to them, 'Hey girls, glad to see you. Glad you waited for us.' The cowboys defaulted into their mode for rounding up gentled cattle, and the day ended without a hitch." My waggling boot knocked over a jar of pencils.

What had surprised me even more is that when the babies of those heifers grew up, they weren't afraid of us either. Their mamas did the cowboys' jobs. Training became twice as easy. The whole program fed on itself and, little by little, year by year, required less energy. We had next to no runaways. The success still warmed me. I had shaken the dice and thrown them on the table. Lucky me. They had come up a seven.

"Herd behavior modification training I called it," I said to Les. "And I think it might just work on a herd of wild horses." I scooped up the pencils and returned them to the jar.

A pause filled the phone line. I could almost see Les's questioning expression. Maybe he was thinking about herds of mustangs having lived their whole life wild. Would they respond to such a program? You could argue that we wouldn't be training the horses from the time they were colts. Or argue that we could bait them with grain. But when horses are full, fat, and happy, they won't follow a feed truck. And what if you have to lead them across a river? How do you bait them then? We needed to make friends with the horses like we did with the cattle so they would do our bidding.

Finally Les said, "Call me a Missourian, because you'll have to show me that one."

His reaction came as no surprise. Cowboys, neighbors, friends, and colleagues all hailed from Missouri when I told the gentling cattle story. One neighbor south of Lazy B had the wildest bunch of cattle that time and time again ran away. After each incident, this frustrated guy would pound in a piece of fence here, another piece there in an attempt to contain the animals until pretty soon he had the most nonsensical fencing ever created. I went to him and explained the program, how it was foolproof, and how he could do it. "That's a bunch of shit," he said.

Telling Les about the herd behavior modification program

increased my confidence that wild horses would respond to it. Cocky me. For all I knew, Dayton and I were standing on the drawbridge of an air castle that was about to dump us in the swampy moat. Maybe Les thought so too, but he didn't let on. He told me who to call in the BLM's Wild Horse Division. They would be the ones with information about the current state of affairs and the ones who could authorize a sanctuary. At least that's what he thought.

"I'll give them a call and let them know that you're mostly a reasonable man." He chuckled and hung up with a promise to let me know when travels brought him near Lazy B. I promised to introduce him to our gentled cattle.

The conversation with Les set off a chain reaction of activity. I felt like a spider flinging out filaments that would somehow get woven into a web. I half expected my partners to resist the far-out idea of creating a wild horse sanctuary, but they readily stamped their approval on it. Phone calls to the BLM were being returned, conversations lengthening, and support growing. Dayton Hyde made friends in the South Dakota state tourism office. They liked his idea of putting two or three hundred wild horses on his small ranch and opening it up to tourists. The BLM chimed in with a desire to partner with the state. Over many meetings and cups of coffee, we hammered out a document that gave birth to the Institute of Range and American Mustang, a nonprofit organization designed to ensure the longevity of a sanctuary, protect the horses, and preserve the land.

Then there was the Bureau of Indian Affairs. Of the thirty-five thousand acres that made up the old Arnold Ranch, nine thousand were leased, half from the Rosebud Sioux Indian Tribe and half from the Bureau of Indian Affairs, which meant we needed permission from each group to graze wild horses on their land. I decided to first pay a visit to the person I knew best, Stan Whipple, the range conservationist employed by the Rosebud Sioux Tribe who was responsible for relations with our ranch. He loved our plan, circulated it to the right people, and within a week the tribe had granted us approval. Stan followed up with a fair warning. "Don't be surprised if you get static from the BIA. They never agree with anything we do." I decided it best to drive the short part of an hour up to the Bureau of Indian Affairs office in Mission, South Dakota, and meet with our contact, a Mr. Roger Running Horse. Since we would be working with the BIA long-term, a personal relationship couldn't hurt. John Pitkin accompanied me.

A slender man with an engaging smile, Mr. Running Horse greeted us warmly. "I heard talk of the old Arnold Ranch becoming a wild horse sanctuary. Quite exciting," he said. His openness fanned our enthusiasm and we eagerly rolled out our plans.

"I need to have all this in writing so I can present it to my supervisor over in the Pine Ridge office," said Mr. Running Horse. "It may take a week or two to get approval, but we'll get it done."

John and I left Roger Running Horse's office assuming we had a new ally in our pocket and pleased to have avoided any negativity.

I was lucky if I spent three or four nights in the same bed. Between the blowing and going, I waited for the ranch purchase to close. The banking machinery chugged along in reverse, giving rumors an opportunity to spread like a swarm of no-see-ums. John reported that beer talk at the local bar was pondering the crazy Arizonan buying up ranches left and right in the Sand Hills and aiming to turn the old Arnold Ranch into some sort of sanctuary for three or four thousand mustangs. I could just hear it.

"Sweet Jesus, those horses will be spread over three counties."

"I can see it now. They'll come blastin' through the backyard and Mama will start screaming her roses got trampled."

"Crazy fellow. What's he thinking? Hasn't even weathered a winter yet."

"Yep, when a dang nor'wester blows through, he'll be chasing those damn mustangs up and down the river and hollering for help. He's settin' himself up for big trouble."

I didn't pay too much attention to what people said behind me or to me unless they got in my face, like the field rep for an insurance company who caught up with me one afternoon on the Rex Ranch. At the time, insurance companies were pushing ranch mortgages and three had offered to furnish one for the Rex Ranch. One of the companies had hired this fellow now standing in front of me, an ex-rancher who I knew had gone broke. He claimed his company heard I was putting a wild horse sanctuary on the Rex Ranch.

"If you go ahead with it," he said, loud enough for anyone within ten feet to hear, "you'll be denied a mortgage with us and probably every other company out there as well."

It was all I could do not to say, buddy, you don't know shit from wild honey. Instead, I reminded him in the same forthright tone that he and his cohorts were in the banking business and I was in the ranching business and maybe we should each stick to what we knew best. The subject never surfaced again.

Overall, I couldn't complain about how things were spinning together. Yet through the hubbub, a little voice managed to assert itself. Go see the wild horses, it urged. Learn from the experts who handle them. Ask all the important questions. Would the handlers think training and gentling over a thousand horses a possible feat? How did they sort the horses? What kind of branding methods did they use? Did the horses move easily between corrals? Did the herds have renegades or protectors, and how did those horses behave? What criteria made a horse adoptable? How much did they eat?

The best place to be a student was the National Wild Horse and Burro Center at Palomino Valley, twenty-five miles outside Reno, Nevada. Before I left, I called my son, Alan Jr., who had been a sounding board from day one of this journey, and asked him if he would fly up to South Dakota to spend a week on the ranch with John. I wanted his take on the ranch as wild horse sanctuary. Al had logged enough years on horseback to be considered a full-fledged cowboy, even though he had opted not to join the family ranching business. He could stay in the doublewide and not be influenced by my presence. He readily agreed. So in mid-August Alan Jr. left the dry heat of Tucson, bound for the humid air of South Dakota, and I rumbled out Lazy B's ranch road, turned left, and pointed the pickup toward the Silver State.

CHAPTER FOUR

Palomino Valley

I smelled the horses before I saw them. Their pungent, wild scent filled the cab. When I pulled into Palomino Valley, I understood why. Horses, horses, and more horses stood and rested in a maze of corrals that stretched behind a main office.

At the far end of the parking lot a long semitrailer, the kind used to haul livestock, was backing up against the loading chute attached to a corral fence. I stepped out of the pickup and heard the truck's low purr. Because of the angle of the sun, the scene played out in silhouettes. A driver came around and clanged open the truck's back gate, then pounded a club against the trailer's metal side. A horse's nose poked out. The driver yelled and banged some more. A shadowed mustang emerged and ran down the chute into the corral. A string of horses followed. The beat of hooves on metal drowned out the motor. Within minutes, forty horses or so huddled in a far corner of the corral. The driver slammed the truck gate shut.

Well, no big deal there, I thought, walking toward the office. I'd be able to handle that. I had unloaded cattle from trucks hundreds of times.

"How ya do, Mr. Day?" A tall, sun-weathered man in a plaid shirt and bolo tie stood up and leaned over a desk piled with neat stacks of paperwork to shake my hand. He motioned for me to take a seat. "Glad you could join us. We don't get too many people expressing such interest in wild horses," he said, leaning back in his chair.

For the next thirty minutes, we chatted about the process of sorting horses and details of the adoption program.

"Now, let me ask you this," I said, eager to get to the most important question. "If you had a ranch in South Dakota covered in a thick, healthy grass, would you want to turn wild mustangs out on it? Or would you run a hundred miles the other way to keep from doing it?"

The manager folded his arms and stared out the window. "If it were me," he said, "I might think double hard about how much time I'd want to spend chasing horses. You could end up learning every inch of that property trying to round up horses that don't want to be handled."

I briefly described the cattle training started on Lazy B. "Think it might work with a bunch of mustangs?"

The question earned me a curious look. "Can't say I know much about training cattle. But I do know wild horses don't want to do anyone's bidding—yours, mine, or the best blue-ribbon cowboy west of the Mississippi. You might bait them with hay and get them to follow you, but the minute you turn those animals out on the range, they revert to their wild ways. Guaranteed."

The conversation turned to horse care and maintenance. A bottle with a handwritten label perched on a shelf caught my attention.

"Tell me about that euthanizing solution up there," I said. The manager looked over at the cluttered shelf. "Is that something I would need to keep on hand?"

"We have that by prescription only," he said. "We do our best to avoid using it. If a horse kicks or jumps and knocks the syringe out of your hand, you don't want to get stabbed. It works its magic without discretion. My suggestion is to use a good old Colt .45. That's our preference when a horse is sick or injured and needs to be put down. It's much safer." I used that same method on the rare occasions when I had to euthanize a ranch horse.

"So do you ever try to train horses in the corrals?" I asked.

The manager pointed out the window. "Those two fellows can answer your questions about horse handling. They pretty much do it all day."

"Well then, I'll go have a chat with them."

"Hope it all works out for you," said the manager, extending a hand.

Outside, hot air pumped against me. I pushed my hat down and followed a corral fence constructed of solid metal tubing and extending a good seven feet high. Too high for a horse to jump, too solid to be knocked over. The handlers stood near a corrugated tin shack, sweat streaked on their shirts. One was smoking and the other drinking a Coke.

"Hey there," I said, and introduced myself. The fellow with the Coke, named Red, probably after the color of his hair, had worked at Palomino Valley for about two years. Roy, the other cowboy, had been there almost as long, having come over from a ranch in Wyoming.

"So what in the world brings an Arizona cattle rancher up here?" Red said.

I gave the lowdown on the sanctuary. "Problem is I've never handled wild horses. Thought I might learn a thing or two from you boys." A look of pride flashed across their faces.

Roy said, "Well, one thing's for sure. They won't let you get bored. You'll be too busy riding in circles."

"Yeah, these suckers, they'll run five miles without drawing a deep breath," said Red. He took the last swig of soda and aimed at a garbage can five feet away. The can swished in with a clank. "They'll run around you, away from you, in every crazy direction."

"After you work with them for a while, do they start to respect you? Maybe trust you a little bit?" I asked.

Red snorted. "Hell no. You sure ain't been around a bunch of wild horses. You expect the ornery cusses to do one thing, and they get in their dang head to do the opposite."

"Remember Jimmy?" said Roy, slapping Red on the arm. "He went to shutting a gate in front of a renegade red roan mare. That bitch hit the gate at a full run and wham, Jimmy caught it right in his face. Shit, he was ironed out. Lost part of his front teeth on that little charge. Took most of his desire to be a cowboy right out of him."

Red snorted. "Yeh, Jimmy. He's probably still bartending in Reno." The boys got a good laugh out of that one.

Red eyed me. "Just so you know, your ranch is gonna be like what you see here. The pretty horses, they get adopted right off the bat. We end up with the ugly, wild ones that no one wants, and they are damn difficult to care for. You say you're thinking about taking care of several thousand of these scrounges. Well, I say, mister, are you crazy or just misguided?"

I gulped down the reality check. Crazy, yes. Misguided, I sure hoped not.

By the time we started walking to the corrals, I knew that the boys believed if the South Dakota ranch didn't have tall, iron fences, say seven feet tall, the horses would be scattered from hell to high water across the neighbors' pastures. Horses could be baited with hay, but no way in the world could they be trained. These cowboys stood on a different dance floor than the one I was hoping to two-step on, but it didn't surprise me all that much. Yet, since they spent each day working with wild horses and had expertise I lacked, I felt compelled to consider their opinions. Red pointed out the small corral holding the new arrivals, the ones I had seen being unloaded earlier, and suggested I go take a look.

I walked through several empty corrals, opening and closing gates until I reached the small one. Most of the horses had their heads down, munching on the hay strewn across the ground, and took little notice of me. They had congregated into family groups of seven or nine. Red said they had ridden two hundred miles in the semitrailer before being unloaded on these foreign grounds. I leaned my arms against the corral tubing, stood still, and observed. It must have seemed like a seven-course meal served at a desert oasis compared to the overgrazed, drought-ridden range they had come from. They didn't have a chance to wash up and put on their best duds. To tell the truth, they looked ratty, with long hair and dull, lusterless coats.

A brown mare with a swooping neck and black mane with a forelock that hung halfway down her nose stood near me, her light-brown foal next to her. She wasn't terribly big, maybe fourteen hands high. Dried streaks of sweat covered the outline of her ribs and her underbelly. The foal, probably about a month old, walked around his mama and came broadside to me. With legs poking out like skinny sticks from his torso, he already showed the results of overgrazing and feed shortage. He nuzzled his mother for a drink of milk but, finding none, walked away and picked at some of the loose hay on the ground.

Many of the other horses looked like they too had had a workout. How many miles did they have to run from the hated helicopter to be marked with such defined sweat streaks? A terrifying run, followed by jail. At least they were fed well in jail.

"Fun will start tomorrow," said Red, coming up behind me. "The vet pulls in around ten. We'll run the bunch up the chute and get them vaccinated and branded. You're welcome to watch."

I was eager to see the interaction between man and animal and get a glimmer of whether or not I could work with mustangs. Even though everyone had told me in one way or another that I wouldn't be able to do it, something deep inside of me said that I could. Yes, these horses seemed different from those I had known. They looked different, too, and they had lived such a different life than the ranch horses I grew up with and had worked with all my life. I would have to accept that I wouldn't have the same relationships with wild horses that I had with my ranch horse friends like Chico and Aunt Jemima, Blackberry and Saber. And certainly not like Little Joe. Now there was a horse that grew up acting more like a dog than a horse.

I still remember the first day I met Little Joe. Jim Brister was riding in the back of the pickup, instead of on his horse or in the cab next to Leroy McCarty, the ranch foreman who was driving the pickup in from the east pasture. At first I thought maybe Jim had hurt himself, because even by age ten, I knew he felt his best on a horse, not in a four-wheeled vehicle. Leroy pulled the truck up next to the barn. I abandoned chasing an imaginary bandit around headquarters buildings and ran over to greet them.

A head popped up next to Jim and a foal plopped its nose awkwardly over the truck bed's side. "Who's this?" I said, petting the baby's fine, soft hairs. A tuft of gray mane stood up between his ears. The foal blinked at me.

"We found him in the pasture circling around his mama, dead on the ground," Jim said. He jumped out of the truck and swung down the back gate. "She must have just died 'cuz the coyotes didn't get to her yet." He reached in and pulled the colt by his legs, then lifted him and set him on the ground.

The baby's loss pricked my heart, especially since the other broodmares would be reluctant to adopt him. He stood there, skinny legs splayed, looking out of sorts. I put my arm around his neck and gave him a hug.

Jim said, "Go get a bottle of warm milk from your mother. You can feed him down in the corral." I ran to the barn to get the bottle with the nipple that we used to feed orphans. My mom always left warm milk on the kitchen counter. I dipped the bottle below the layer of cream and filled it.

For the next three months, I fed Little Joe a bottle at least once a day, sometimes twice if I wasn't in school. Gradually, he came into his coloring. He was a blue roan, handsome even at a young age, with a peppered light gray on his flanks and darker hairs around hips and neck. His nose, mane, and eyes were black. I don't remember who started calling him Joe, but it didn't take long before he was known around the ranch as Little Joe. And was he known.

When I went down to the corral, he would be there waiting for me, bobbing his head and flipping his tail. He would watch me unlatch and swing open the gate, then he'd skip out, come to a stop, and look at me to see what the plan of action was. We'd wander around the ranch, his nose resting on my shoulder when content or nudging me along when I dawdled.

If I walked into the bunkhouse, Little Joe tried to follow. Bug, our cook, would yell, "Get that damn horse out of here," and the two of us would hightail it out before we found out if the frying pan Bug held was headed for one of us or the stove. Out in the yard, I'd push my shoulder against Little Joe's. "Don't take it personally. He's that way with a lot of people."

I was so accustomed to having Little Joe out of the corral that I wouldn't think to put him back in there. When I ran inside the house, Little Joe would wait for me in the yard. "Take your damn horse and put him in the corral," my dad would holler if he saw Little Joe grazing around the front walk. I'd come out and put a hand on Little Joe's neck and lead him back to the corral. He never looked happy when I shut the gate. "I'll come get you later," I'd say. He would push his nose over the corral tubing for a last rub. Sometimes I climbed on Little Joe and let him take me for a ride wherever he wanted to go, but I knew that he shouldn't have much weight on him until he was older. Almost every day, I fed him extra grain and watched him grow. And he watched me grow. It seemed like we consistently stood at eye level with each other.

The summer of my thirteenth year I was eager to have my own cow horse that I could ride out on the range. I had outgrown

Chico, though I still loved him and always would. By then Little Joe, having been fed quite well, had become big and strong and was ready to break. Since he was my horse, it was my responsibility to do that. When I went to break him, I assumed he would partner with me like he always did.

It proved quite the challenge, however, to break him into our new relationship. He wanted a partnership where he had at least 50 percent of the say. He didn't mind a saddle, but he did mind being given directions. If I wanted him to turn, he continued straight ahead. When I snapped the reins for him to gallop, he kicked at me with a back foot or turned his head and nipped at my knee. "You're spoiled," I said to him one day in the corral in a moment of frustration. He wasn't bucking, but he wasn't doing much of anything I asked him. The dry June heat and our individual wills to win made us both cranky.

After a month or so, Little Joe wearied of fighting every day. You're the boss, he acknowledged, giving in to the pressure of the reins or my knees. I'll follow your orders. "That's a boy," I said, my arms around his neck. I looked into his eyes and saw friendship. "Now let's go round up some cows."

When the sun rose on a day the open range called, Little Joe and I would be one of the first to saddle up. He had a shorter gait than the other horses and a rough trot, so it was tiring riding him all day, but at thirteen that didn't bother me in the least. I had my own horse and we were a working team. Besides, if I leaned forward and pitched him the slack, he could hit a dead run faster than almost any of the other ranch horses, though I didn't yet have the skills to teach him how to stop smoothly. Instead of putting his back legs forward and lowering his hips, he would bounce to a stop on stiff front legs. Plus, he was kind of a sneaky guy. When we rode near a fence or tree or shrub, he would veer into them with the subtlest of movements and scrape my leg against them. More than a few times, I had to pull out prickly pear and cholla needles that pierced my chaps and jeans. One day, I had enough. The next time Little Joe tried to pull his shenanigans, I whacked him a good one on the neck. After that, he behaved. It was all part of our give-and-take relationship.

One of the best times I had with Little Joe was at Carey's Camp in New Mexico, a horse camp for kids and teens. It was the summer after I broke him. I persuaded Leroy to haul Little Joe the 150 miles up to the camp. By then Little Joe was quite a good reining horse and could turn on a dime. We participated in bareback and saddle races, pole bending and barrel races, and made a haul on blue ribbons. We were the envy of our peers, most of whom had to ride camp horses. I returned to Lazy B feeling like a full-grown cowboy.

That fall, as a high school freshman, I spent more time playing football and chasing girls than riding Little Joe. But when we connected, with me in the saddle and the two of us out on the range, we picked up where we had left off. When I went to college, my dad let other cowboys ride him. I'd come home on breaks and summer vacations and there would be Little Joe, head alert, waiting for me to come down to the corral to say hello and give him some loving. It was as much a part of my welcome home as hugs from my family. When I graduated from college and returned to the ranch to work, Little Joe was middle-aged. On the days I rode him, we'd look each other in the eye. I'd see contentment, enthusiasm, and the steadfast pledge of friendship. "That's a boy," I'd say at the end of those special days, one arm hooked around his neck and the other pouring out a little extra grain. When he grew too old for long days on the range chasing cattle, he retired to a pasture on Lazy B where he had leisurely days hanging out in the sun. He died in his late twenties.

When I think back on all the horses I've bonded with and ridden over the years, the blue roan with the big heart always brings a smile to my face.

I wouldn't find any Little Joes at Palomino Valley, but maybe I would get some insight into the wild horses. So the next morning I returned. Red and Roy and a third handler were saddling their horses and greeted me with a wave. The herd had been moved to a rectangular feed corral that looked to be about half an acre with gates in the middle of each side. I wandered along the perimeter, looking for a good viewing spot. The horses milled about, some pushing their noses into the hay spread on the ground. I spotted the foal walking, his head more alert than yesterday. Maybe the alfalfa hay was helping his mama produce more milk. An occasional grunt and snort floated through the air. I settled on a spot close to where an old dun rested. A jagged scar ran from hip socket to flank and one eye was half-closed.

A handler opened a corral gate on the side opposite me, and Red and Roy and another cowboy, mounted on their horses, entered. The gate remained open. Their mission was to drive the horses through that gate into a smaller corral and eventually into an alley that led to the working chute where the vet awaited. The cowboys' presence seemed to trigger an alarm only the horses could hear. Ears pricked forward. Nostrils widened. The mustangs started to skitter and shift, some prancing in place, others wheeling back and forth in quick movements. A thin palomino ran for the far corner. The horses bumped against each other turning to follow her. The dun struggled to push herself up and join the group. Her one eye filled with fear.

The herd migrated into a huddle. Panicked heads jostled over and under each other, blind to anything but trying to find safety. A bay stallion stood at the edge of the herd eyeing the approaching cowboys. He shook his head up and down and let loose a high-pitched squeal. The dun struggled, pulled herself up, ran on three legs over to the group, and wedged her way into the inner circle.

Red started trotting toward the group to flush it out of the corner while the other two cowboys got in position to wing the horses through the open gate. The bay was the first to break. He stretched out his neck and charged toward the opposite corner. Within seconds, the rest of the herd noticed and took off behind him. Roy and the other cowboy stood their ground as the mustangs ran toward them. Ten yards in front of the cowboys, the stallion paused, glanced at the gate, then put his head down and raced along the corral fence past the gate and the men. The herd followed its leader. Dust rose around the cowboys as the horses thundered past. The frightened animals huddled in the far corner, heads down and ears back.

"Aw right," yelled Red, circling his arm in the air. "Let's give it another go, boys."

He approached the herd. The horses broke and ran. Missed the gate. Rehuddled. Roy and the other wrangler shifted their horses into position. Red came at the herd again, and again the horses ran. They bunched in the corner, sides heaving. The hot sun reflected off the shiny sweat forming on their hides. The cowboys went at it again. Clouds of dust swirled in a vortex of increasing frustration. The conflict of wills between horse and man hung in the air, as strong as the smell of alfalfa and wild animal. I knew eventually the men would prevail because they always did in this world, but that didn't mean the scene unfolding in front of me was easy to watch. Forty-eight hours ago, these creatures had been running and playing and living on open range. Now here they were, a pod of fear and flight, moving deeper into a process they didn't understand.

"You hardheaded sons of bitches. How many times is it going to take for you to see the gate?" Red wiped his forehead with the sleeve of his shirt. If the gate had been in the corner, the cowboys' job would have been far easier.

"Go slow boys. Hold 'em and let 'em see the gate," yelled Red, pushing at the back of the bunch. This time, as if telepathically communicating, the three lead horses stopped right in front of the gate. The rest of the mustangs pulled up behind them. Some looked over at the corral on the other side, others watched the cowboys in front of and behind them.

The skinny palomino was closest to the opening. She crouched on her hind legs and in one smooth, powerful movement jumped through the open space and landed in the next corral. The other horses saw she survived. They rushed the gate at once, trying to crowd through like subway riders boarding a train at rush hour. The gate jammed, but with a bit of jostling the first line of horses emerged unscathed. The rest filtered through without a hitch.

The three cowboys rode through and a wrangler slammed the gate shut. I climbed higher on the fence to see over into this new corral. It looked to be to be half the size of the large arena. The horses did four more wind sprints from corner to corner, then ran around its circumference and peeled through the open gate. A handler slammed the gate shut. This time the cowboys stayed behind, a good idea, as the horses were tightly bunched, crushed against the sides of the corral. They dismounted and tied their horses to the corral tubing. By the time I found my way closer to the action, Red, Roy, and three other wranglers stood on the tubing, each holding long poles with tattered white flags tied at the end. They waved the flags at the horses in an effort to get them to go toward the alley. The horses looked around, nervous and confused, edging away from the pesky flags.

It continued to be slow-going and clumsy. No horse wanted to be first in the alley. Shouts and snorts punctured the oppressive air. Horses' heads bobbed against each other. The cowboys' body language spoke of tension and frustration.

From the alley, the mustangs would funnel into a chute the width of one horse. Once in the chute, each horse would be pushed into a hydraulic squeeze chute that clamped around the animal and rendered it immobile so the attending vet could brand, vaccinate, worm, and if need be, castrate. A logical, well-planned system. We used a similar system at Lazy B. Once we trained our cattle, minimal chaos and friction attended the process. The cattle understood what we wanted from them and obeyed. It became far easier on all of us.

These horses, however, with wary eyes and flicking tails, were not gentled or trained. No one had talked to them and introduced them to their foreign surroundings. They had been kidnapped and deposited in a culture that was as foreign to them as a suit and tie on Wall Street would be to me. Consequently, the cowboys' job was five times harder than it might be if the horses knew the system.

The vet had parked his truck near the squeeze chute, the final destination for each horse before being released into a large corral. I watched the pull and tug of the cowboys and horses and reflected on my background of training cattle. Could I train a group of horses like these to follow my orders and not rebel at every step? My intuition—or was it my ego—told me I could. I did know there was a less stressful way to handle these horses.

I walked over to say hello to the vet and secure an unobtrusive place from which to watch the grand finale.

"Hey there," I said. The vet looked up from organizing an assortment of instruments. "I'm a spectator at this tango. Tell me where you want me to go, so I won't step on any toes. Or get my toes stepped on."

"Let's see. I'll be working here, around the head of the horses," said the vet, pointing to the end of the squeeze chute. "When we release them, they'll go straight into that corral." He pointed. "If you stand behind the chute, you'll be good. Just make sure you don't stand in front of it. These guys will be eager to get out and they'll run you over."

From behind the chute, I had a decent view of the escalating chaos.

The horses had entered the alley, five to six abreast, with the leaders straining to get into the crowding pen that funneled down to the chute. Roy closed the gate behind eight horses in the pen, leaving the rest of the horses in the alley. Red and the other wrangler dismounted and left their horses in the third corral. They continued on foot, working safely on the outside of the alley and crowding pen, as well as the narrow chute. It was awkward work.

They leaned over the corral rails, shouted at the confused, frightened horses, jabbed them in the ribs with long sticks, slapped their hands on their backs, and literally shoved them forward. At least they weren't allowed to use hot shots, painful electric shocks given to animals. These cowboys were doing their best while trying to avoid the worst-case scenario: a horse rearing up in the chute. If a horse rears and tips over backward, he becomes like a beetle on his back. Stuck. To avoid injury or even death by trampling, the rest of the chute has to be emptied so that the cowboys can climb in and pull him upright. That situation is not good for horse or wrangler.

I watched Red shut one of the gates in the chute to prevent a sorrel from backtracking. The horse bumped her back end against the hard tubing and stood still for a moment. Red hollered at her and pushed her from behind. She tried to turn her head but couldn't move it much. There was nowhere to go but forward. I could almost feel her resignation. The trauma of the morning, added to the events of the past few days, had siphoned much of her will.

I had seen horses lose their will. Sometimes it never returned. Back in my early teens, Jim Brister, one of the Lazy B cowboys, taught me a major lesson about a horse's will. Jim was the most respected horse breaker on our ranch, not to mention southern Arizona, for the fifty years he worked there. We were out cowboying on Lazy B, and I was riding Sally, a pretty horse, big and strong but gentle in nature. I had placed a hackamore, a bitless bridle, on her nose to train her. Big cotton reins ran from the hackamore into my hands. My fourteen-year-old arms felt sore from pulling the reins on the side I wanted her to turn toward. Every time I pulled one way, she put her head around the other way and stiffened her neck so I couldn't budge her. She was winning the contest of wills and making it difficult to help round up the cattle. My cussing would have embarrassed my mother. I could see Jim watching us. After some time, he rode over and suggested trading horses. It sounded like the idea of the century.

With a large, athlete's body and chiseled, strong face topped with a well-worn black hat, Jim looked like he was born on a horse. He mounted Sally, who was not yet fully grown. He hadn't ridden one hundred yards when he reached up, grabbed the rein near the headstall and jerked her nose clear around to touch his knee. He pulled so hard she crumpled to the ground. Jim stepped from the saddle, clamped his foot on the bend of her neck and held her nose up almost waist high. She struggled to get up. Jim took the reins and began whipping her nose. She squealed and swam her legs through the air, but he kept her pinned. The reins slapped and slapped against her nose. He whipped her until she urinated on the ground. I sat on Jim's horse not more than twenty feet away, my stomach in my throat, barely comprehending what was happening in front of me.

From that moment, Sally never resisted being pulled to the right or the left. In fact, she never resisted much of anything. Although I loved Jim for many reasons, I never liked his horse-health-be-damned school of training. Yet he was my role model for training horses. It would take me until I trained Saber ten years later to finally figure out a gentler method of teaching a horse and earning its respect.

I watched a cowboy jab the bay stallion with a pole to make him jump into the hydraulic clamp. His struggling proved useless. The vet started to do his thing. He shaved patches on the horse's neck and hip, then pressed the branding iron, cooled to thirty below zero, against the bare skin for thirty seconds or so. The hair on the frozen skin would grow back white. He then moved to the front of the horse and inspected his teeth. He wrote something on a clipboard, presumably an estimate of the horse's age, his color, and if he knew, where the horse had been captured. Next he inserted a tube with worm medicine down the horse's throat, then vaccinated for disease. Castration was next. The vet cut off the end of the scrotum and pulled down the testicles until two cords were visible. He clamped the cords to stop the bleeding, picked up a scalpel, and sliced off the testicles. The horse shook slightly. The surgery took about ten minutes and the proceedings before it another ten minutes. The horse now had a social security card of sorts and was part of the government's system.

One by one the horses moved through the chute. When they exited, they ran to the far end of the corral and shook their heads as if to regain their senses and recover from the trauma they had just endured. As mates were released, the families—some still together from the open ranges, others formed since arriving yesterday—reconvened. They had entered a new world. They never again would be wild on open range.

As I stood and watched the process, I noticed a furrow in the dirt running from in front of the squeeze chute to a gate at the opposite side of the corral. At first I didn't understand why the furrow would be right there, but then it dawned on me that the depression was from a horse being dragged out of the chute. And the only reason a horse would be dragged out is if it died. The vision of the three dead heifers at Lazy B came flooding back to me.

The vet took a break and I walked over to him.

"I see you had to drag a few out of here," I said, pointing to the furrow.

"Occasionally we lose one," he said without looking up.

Right there, I placed my bet on the table that a herd of wild horses could be trained without being traumatized. I had done it with cattle, I would do it with horses. Same movie script, different actors. We could transform their fear, get them to cooperate and follow directions. Once trained, we would show them the gate, and they would go through it. We would show them the alley, and they would file in like well-behaved grade school students and wait their turn. We would vaccinate them and turn them out of the squeeze chute calmly. They would not view us as the enemy and the scene would be devoid of this palpable stress. There was no reason to spoil an animal's spirit with force and fear. I resolved then and there that I would help these captured horses and give them the next best thing to the life they had once known. That voice inside of me was right. It was time to work with wild horses.

A week later I flew up to South Dakota. Al Jr. and I sat on the porch of the doublewide watching the prairie tuck itself in to sleep. Al had fallen in love with the ranch and everything about it. When I asked him if he could envision a sanctuary on the land, he said, "It's a crazy idea putting wild horses out here. But if anyone can pull it off, it's you, Dad."

The flock of wild turkeys waddled into sight, crossed the ranch road, and headed for the elm tree. One by one, they spread their wings and flapped into the tree. Since my first night on the ranch, I had watched them go through this routine. I wondered if they slept on the same branch every night.

"Hey, I want to show you something," my son said, getting up from the step. I followed him across the lawn. Only a thin line of light hung on the horizon. "Stand under the elm and look out over the pond," he said. I moved next to the trunk and pressed a hand against its rough bark. Al stayed back. I was about to tell him to come take in the view when he clapped three times. The tree rustled, like sheets in a bed. I heard the drops hit the ground before I felt the warm liquid slide down the back of my neck.

"What the . . ." I was covered in turkey poop.

Al burst out laughing. "Gotcha."

I pulled out my handkerchief. Now how on earth did he figure that one out? It was one of those questions that never got answered.

CHAPTER FIVE

Two Cowboys Corral Congress

The banking gears continued to grind through the loan process. I was trying to be patient, but by golly, it was hard. Since we had not heard from Roger Running Horse I decided to drive to his office, hoping to speed the process along. He met me with his usual big smile and a warm greeting. "My supervisor is on vacation but she should be back soon and we'll get those plans in front of her before long," he reassured me. I left his office mildly disappointed but with hopes of future approval.

I couldn't start making improvements on the old Arnold Ranch until it officially became the new Day Ranch, so in the meantime, in an effort to learn the trade secrets of Sand Hills ranching, I spent quite a little time chatting with neighbors. I wanted to determine what normal hay production should be. The Arnold Ranch produced one ton per acre, which for the area was substandard. I submitted soil and hay samples to a lab and discovered that the three thousand acres of hay-producing meadow were deficient in phosphorous and the hay was low in protein. Horses would require healthy hay. They also needed stronger corrals and more drinking water on the range. I was eager to get going on these projects. Finally, the phone rang. On a windy day, with silver-lined clouds scudding across the South Dakota sky and the sunflowers of mid-September in bloom, I signed on the dotted line.

On the drive back to the ranch, I inhaled the sweet scent of freshly cut fields and thought about the horses. I now had a home to offer them, a safe harbor where they could roam and graze. Tomorrow John and I would start remodeling that home. Even if the horses never came, the place needed major upgrades. I turned onto the dirt road, hit a pothole, and bumped my head against the pickup's roof. Yeah, the road. Better get on that one soon, too, or the horses would have to unload at the edge of the state highway and hoof it to the ranch.

I bounced past the gnarled old fence post and the start of the ranch, my ranch. I was the caretaker now, the one responsible for every pothole, fence post, and blade of grass. I had set these 35,000 acres atop the 45,000 acres of the Rex Ranch, which sat atop the 198,000 acres of Lazy B. For the next five miles, this agrarian monolith loomed in front of me, weighed down with cattle, investors, debt, and uncertainty. I could no longer see the grass waving or the hills beckoning. Trepidation wormed through my confidence like some nasty alien in a video game gobbling up all the good guys. I pulled into the yard feeling slightly sick. A cloud cast its blobby shadow over the truck, floated toward the faded barn, and disappeared behind it.

Oh my God. What had I done?

I had been raised on lectures portraying debt as evil, yet here I was dancing with the devil himself. I slumped in my seat like a guy who just became engaged to the love of his life and contracts an acute case of marriage remorse.

A patch of sunlight spilled through the windshield, warming my fingers still curled around the steering wheel. Somewhere deep inside, resolve poked its head out. Fearless, it grew. I grabbed onto it. I had endured droughts, lost money on cattle, even crashed an airplane and almost died, but those receding tides never left me high and dry. They always returned and deposited good fortune at my feet. I'd dig in my heels and see this journey through to the end. My horse Little Charlie Brown use to do that—dig in his heels. Remembering him inspired and calmed me.

He was a little guy, a bay horse with white stockings, not very tall but solidly built. A white streak ran the length of his nose and dribbled down one nostril. He had a gentle demeanor but could be as lazy as a teenager. Except when he got around cattle. Then he became all business. If he and I rode behind a herd of cattle and a cow slowed down, he'd follow that cow, reach down, and bite her right above the hock. If I didn't pull him off, he would raise her leg and hold it up like a bulldog. The cow would bawl in pain and try to run forward. With Little Charlie, you could make good time driving cattle because they knew if they didn't hotfoot it, they'd get chomped on. But he'd never bite a baby calf, only nudge it.

His real talent, though, was his unbelievable strength. I'd saddle him up, throw my rope around a bull, a tractor, or whatever needed moving, then dally up and tell Little Charlie to pull. He could drag a full-grown bull from one corral to another. I learned that the best way to load a recalcitrant cow or horse into a trailer was to run a rope from the stubborn animal through the trailer, back to front, then dally it to Little Charlie. He'd crouch his back end and push with all fours like he was going for the gold in tug-of-war. The animal in tow practically popped into the trailer. He should have been named Samson. Where he got that strength, and for his size, I don't know. Some athletes are wired a certain way; some horses are too. You always knew what Little Charlie could do for you, and he did it day in and day out. I had this ranch dallied to my inner saddle horn. Could I drag it with me?

That night, to celebrate the closing, I took the Pitkin family to the Peppermill Steakhouse just over the border in Valentine, Nebraska, where we stuffed ourselves full of prime rib that practically melted in our mouths. John told stories about the ranch with his kids chiming in details. I told stories about ranching in Arizona that left them shaking their midwestern heads. With laughs and giggles, we embarked on an adventure that seemed to have chosen us randomly and united us in the heartland of the country. I had inserted myself in this family and the Sand Hills. I needed to own up to that and not let them down. With the fortitude of Little Charlie Brown, I could do it. By the time we left, I couldn't wait to see what lay over the next hill. I never expected it to lay so far east.

In Arizona no one bothers to look twice at a cowboy. I could walk through Sky Harbor Airport in Phoenix wearing my favorite black Stetson and leather boots without attracting so much as a glance, but standing in the baggage claim of Dulles International Airport outside Washington DC dressed in the same attire, I attracted some blatant body scans. Usually when I traveled here once a year to visit my sister, Sandra, and her husband, John, I did so sans western regalia. The itinerary of this trip, however, demanded an identity statement. The thing about cowboy hats is they don't pack well.

The Wild Horse Division of the BLM had sprung a new mission on Dayton and me. The higher-ups had indicated that a wild horse sanctuary was more than a good idea; it could be a practical solution to the problem of what to do with unadoptable wild horses living in holding facilities. We thought we were headed down easy street until they advised us they didn't have the power to authorize such a venture. "You'll need to get approval from Congress," a representative from Washington stated during a meeting in South Dakota. Congress, huh? Did the BLM really need the approval of its boss, or were the good folks in the agency sending us down the yellow brick road on a bogus journey? It was more likely they didn't want to stand up to Congress so they handed us the script and set us on stage, a tactical cover-your-ass move. But certainly the BLM folk wouldn't underestimate a cowboy, would they? Because a cowboy does what it takes to get the job done, even if that includes personally soliciting politicians.

As luck would have it, Dayton's flight from Oregon was landing twenty minutes after mine. We had agreed to meet near the exit to catch a cab, but signs indicated three exits for taxis and the place was busier than a pub on payday. I stood by a large column and watched for a familiar face in the flow of people.

An older woman passing by leaned over to her husband and pointed behind her. "Did you see that guy back there in the white cowboy hat?"

He looked over his shoulder. "No, why?"

"I think he's famous. I swear I've seen him in a movie."

I looked behind them and, sure enough, bouncing above the crowd was a white cowboy hat with Dayton beneath it.

"Hey partner," Hawk said, slapping me on the back. "Been waiting long?" I could see how someone might mistake him for a movie star. Put an eye patch on him and he could be John Wayne playing Rooster Cogburn.

"I use to have a pair of them boots," said the cab driver, throwing our luggage in the trunk. "Did a bit of wranglin' up in Montana." He explained that was before an injury shoved him off the ranch and pushed him east little by little, farther and farther, until he hit salt water. His nose had a jaunty bent and a scar smiled across the bottom of his chin. He became our captive audience during the rush-hour drive downtown, listening to all the reasons why the government should sponsor a wild horse sanctuary. We had become pretty good at outlining our argument, but a last-minute practice couldn't hurt. We were no longer in laid-back South Dakota or Arizona. Did busy congressmen and -women give you an hour, half hour, or ten minutes?

"Best of luck to you," said the driver. He set my duffel bag on the sidewalk. "Hell of an idea. I'd sign on to wrangle with you if I could." He shook my hand. Was that a standing ovation for our dress rehearsal? I handed him the fare and a healthy tip.

That night over scotch, we reviewed our agenda. We had three days to corral Congress and so far had a whopping four appointments. The empty blocks of time stood out starkly on the calendar, yet they felt more like a blank canvas than a white surrender flag. What pictures would be painted on them had yet to be determined. With over five hundred politicians on our call list, odds were they would be colored with interesting conversations and characters.

Buzzing through congressional offices the next day proved to be a far bigger high than I anticipated. There's something about being a citizen and tapping into the inner workings of government that gives you a different sense of identity. As a rancher, I responded to animals and land and, to some extent, government. Stepping into the heart of national government with the intent of influencing felt like stepping into something far larger than any ranch I had ever managed.

Our quest for the golden legislation started with a senator Dayton knew from Oregon. He listened attentively to the high points of the sanctuary plan—saving the government money, easing the burden of wild horses on the BLM, giving eighteen hundred unadoptable horses a place to live—and extended his support. The representative from Oregon with whom we next met did the same.

The next stop was former Arizona senator Barry Goldwater's office. I had attended the University of Arizona with his son, Mike, who was a good friend of mine. Barry, of course, knew Sandra from their days of crossing political paths in Phoenix. How much pull he would have with Congress, having retired about two years earlier, I had no idea. Barry whistled when he heard the number of horses we might be allotted. He had photographed wild horses on the Navajo reservation and would love to do the same up in the Sand Hills if we ended up with the sanctuary. He would do all he could to help our expectations come to fruition.

After lunch we hit Senator Dennis DeConcini's office. Along with Barry Goldwater, DeConcini had been a huge supporter of my sister when she went through congressional questioning before being appointed a Supreme Court justice. I hadn't seen him since Sandra's inauguration. I had not asked Sandra to contact him on our behalf, nor to contact anybody else, because I knew better than to do that, especially for a personal project like this one. But I did appreciate having a history that opened the door.

"Take a seat and I'll let the senator know you're here." The receptionist pointed to a partially occupied row of chairs across from her desk.

Dayton and I watched people come and go. A young aide whizzed by balancing white paper bags and a tray of drinks. "Hey, real cowboys! Find a parking spot for your horses?" The receptionist rolled her eyes.

"You did tie up the horse to the parking meter?" Dayton said, looking me in the eye.

"Sure did," I said. "Did you feed the meter?"

"Hell no. I thought you did."

I shrugged. "Nope."

"Hope that stallion doesn't kick the attendant who gives him a ticket. Last guy ended up with a few broken ribs."

A woman sitting across from us glanced up from her magazine. The receptionist giggled.

"Alan, good to see you again." Senator DeConcini made us feel like we were walking into his office on a red carpet. We gave him the lowdown on the sanctuary, and he exuded the same excitement as Goldwater. "Listen, I want you to make this office your headquarters," he said. "My staff can help you make appointments and you can use our phones. I'll add a rider on a bill we know is going to pass and I'll make some calls to get the cooperation we need for this to go through." We had just been offered a pot of gold. DeConcini suggested we lunch in the senators' private dining room and ushered us on the underground train reserved for senators that runs between the Capitol and the senate building. After a brief tour of the Capitol, he wished us well and said he'd be in touch.

The next forty-eight hours became a blur of meetings and conversations, most in offices, some in hallways. I had worn-out the heels of cowboy boots on dirt and gravel but never on concrete and marble. Dayton was the appointed poet, painting the plight of wild horses in word pictures and describing the ranches where they would run free. I detailed the sanctuary's business plan. Not one politician found fault with the sanctuary or refused to support it in the form of a future vote. One of my favorite meetings was with Representative Ben Nighthorse Campbell of Colorado, who later became a senator. He owned a ranch and had raised quarter horses; we spent almost two hours swapping horse stories.

Our final meeting ended up being with the head of the Bureau of Land Management's Bob Burford. We had been dealing with lower-level individuals in the Wild Horse Division and so needed to do a sales job on the higher-ups and hoped they would be at the meeting. But they were not present when we arrived. We exchanged pleasantries and got acquainted with Burford.

"Let me call in some people interested in your project," he said. "They know you're here and are eager to meet you." Bingo.

Dayton and I sailed through our presentation. We have this ranch just begging for horses, and you have horses just begging to be turned out. Doesn't solve all your problems, but it solves the issue of what to do with the unadoptable mustangs. Heads nodded. What really caught their attention was when we mentioned the sanctuary would be a great opportunity for news stories that would put the BLM in a positive light. No person or agency in DC turns down good publicity. They reminded us that we needed Congress's approval, and we said we were on our way to getting it.

We finished our tour on schedule and left with more support than we had imagined. Years later, I figured out we could have hired lobbyists. Would it have been more effective? Not at that stage, but maybe later on. I didn't know it at the time, but once you start lobbying, you have to continue to pet that puppy, otherwise it'll run off and a new dog will step in. But it takes more than three days to learn the inner workings of Washington. Sometimes you don't even learn it in four years.

CHAPTER SIX

Hard-Won Approval

In the spring of 1989 I moved into the doublewide, which turned out to be a real pit. The previous owner's presence lingered in the smell of tobacco and brown smoke stains covering ceiling and walls. Sue would have to put her magic touch on the place. I couldn't wait to introduce her to the ranch, have her feel that rush, that high the land offered. Maybe to christen it, we would throw a mattress in the pickup and head off to the grove by the Little White River. She had declined my most recent invitation to visit, saying she had her hands full on Lazy B. Oh well, I thought, eventually she'll get here. In the meantime, I was eager to get acquainted with the ranch, learn its rhythm and language, idiosyncrasies and needs.

Mornings soon became my favorite time. I'd lie in bed listening to chirps and caws and rustling leaves, then brew a pot of coffee and drink a cup on the porch. The wild turkeys would fly down from their perch and feast on a breakfast of grasshoppers. This was our private time, when the ranch and I smiled at each other. John might wander over, mug in hand, or I'd end up in his kitchen, a map of the ranch spread across the table, Debbie planning her day and directing the kids. Before I even took a sip of coffee, five-year-old Megan would be up on my lap. "What are we gonna do today, Alan?" she'd ask, happy with any answer that involved her participation.

In those first months, talking to John was like panning for gold and coming up with a handful of nuggets. I learned that the entire ranch sat atop the Ogallala Aquifer. I made it a point to inspect each of the fifteen operating windmills on the ranch. The first thing I did was taste the freshly pumped water spilling from a pipe into the holding tank. Every well had clear, cool, pure water—ambrosia to a rancher. I could have kept drinking until water spouted from my fingers and toes. Surely the horses would lap up this find. I've been on plenty of ranches where the water tasted salty or left an aftertaste of sulfur or, worse yet, contained gyp water that makes your stomach clench. On Lazy B we had one well that was so corrosive the cook used to claim if you threw a sack of potatoes in the holding tank and left them for a half day, those spuds would peel themselves.

John and I also spent days driving in the pickup or riding horseback to determine where we might need additional wells and water tanks for the horses. I learned that drilling a well was like pushing a straw into a juicy orange. Get Babby Well Drilling Company to haul out a portable well rig and the next day a windmill would be pumping water up from twenty to thirty feet below. I came from country where drilling for water was akin to drilling for oil under the Arctic tundra. First there was talk of drilling. This might last a year or two. Eventually a dowser, commonly known as a water witch, would be summoned to pinpoint the source of underground water. For some folks, water witching is right there with the Ouija board and psychic predictions, but I grew up watching dowsers work their wonders. Most held a forked peach tree branch in each hand and walked along until the tip nose-dived. Beneath that spot, water would be flowing. The good dowsers also could tell you how deep the water ran. Of course, then you had to dig through desert rock. One 750-foot well on Lazy B took two years to drill.

My neighbor Ralph Johnson had the gift of witching. Instead of using a peach branch, he used two welding wires bent at ninety-degree angles. When the two ends crossed, he would declare water. "Gotta drill about five hundred feet," he'd say. Or maybe eight hundred feet. Never was it twenty or thirty feet. Once some underground pipes sprung a leak, but the fiddlefarts who had buried them were long gone and hadn't left the treasure map of where to find them. So I called in Ralph. He located the pipeline within minutes, even tracked the bends in the pipe.

Within weeks, John and I had covered every part of the ranch except the North Ranch, a set of hills north of the Little White River that included three hundred acres of prime meadows and five good grazing pastures. So one morning I suggested to John that we saddle up and go check out that area. Megan begged to come with us. "It's too big a trip, Pumpkin," her father said. "We'll be gone too long." The promise of an afternoon horse ride erased her pout.

I chose a horse from John's string, curried her, and cinched the saddle. The gray clouds hung low enough to touch, and I pulled the collar of my jacket up. "I'm going to have to buy a horse pretty soon," I said. We were trotting through the heifer pasture. John nodded. I didn't need to explain why. A cowboy bonds with his horse in a way nobody else can. It's like having a best friend among a bunch of acquaintances. I had been contemplating bringing up Aunt Jemima, one of my favorite horses on Lazy B, but in the meantime, I wanted a horse that I could call my own. "Any idea where I might look?"

John got a knowing look on his face. "Let me see what I can do, Boss."

We rode on down to Big Nose Flat. A mile and a half away, a sliver of the Little White River reflected the sullen sky. Behind it, the hills of the North Ranch rolled onto the horizon. Everywhere grass rippled, more grass than on all of Lazy B. I felt like a king looking at fine-spun silk. By now, I knew that a smorgasbord of twenty-six different varieties of grass grew on the meadows, and six or seven of those stretched up into the hills. I dismounted at least three or four times before we reached the river, got down on my hands and knees to examine the soil and the plants growing. I viewed the community of plants like the head of a chamber of commerce would see his town. What could that town do if everyone cooperated? How could you evoke that cooperation? At each location, I pulled up a few different seed heads and stalks and stuffed them in the plastic bag I carried in my chaps. Come evening, I would match them to a page in *The Book of Midwestern Grasses*, a gift from a thoughtful neighboring rancher. Instead of a bottle of bourbon or a plate of his wife's warm cookies, he welcomed me with what would soon become my bible.

Our horses splashed across the Little White River and headed up the hill. We stopped on the crest and took in the panorama. Looking south, behind me, was a classic Sand Hills scene. I half expected to see an Indian camp nestled in one of the bends of the Little White with buffalo roaming beyond. Maybe Lewis and Clark had sent a scouting party that stood on this very same hill, curious to encounter the encampment. To the northwest, a meadow stretched before us. A long building stood at its far end.

"That's the old sheep barn," explained John. "Before my time, the ranch had a herd of three thousand sheep. They wintered on this meadow." Well, how about that, the ranch came with a sheep barn. We rode up to take a closer look.

It was a dilapidated structure with sagging corners and weathered wood the color of the clouds. But long, probably as long as a football field. We dismounted and walked inside. A swallow swooped in front of me, stirring the mildewed air. Light filtered through cracks in the rafters and spotlighted weeds in the dirt floor. The gates on the little pens extending the length of the building stood at odd angles.

John said, "I've always been tempted to burn this place down. Not sure what else to do with it."

The place had the feel of Arizona ghost towns I've visited, those once-bustling mining hubs now limp with decay and trafficked by rattlesnakes and tumbleweeds. I could almost hear the ghosts of sheepherders telling their stories of gathering three thousand ewes in here before the blizzard hit. I examined the wooden beams above and around me. Now here was fine, seasoned wood, protected from the piercing summer sun and winter snow and ice.

"Wonder if we could use this wood to build up the corrals back at headquarters," I said.

"Not a bad idea," said John. "But who are you going to get to do the work?" Good question. Available workers in this county seemed scarcer than jobs.

"Tell you what. You get the horse, and I'll scrounge up some labor."

On the way back to headquarters, I mentally reviewed pending projects. Tear down the sheep barn. Rebuild the road. Change pasture fences. Drill five new wells. Paint the barn. Build up the corrals strong enough to hold wild horses. Fertilize the meadows. All good ranching stuff, all stuff that could get done. So why, while riding across this open country, the wind now at my back, was I sinking into a light-gray funk? A few raindrops hit my hands. Today made a week of overcast skies. Maybe I was sun deprived. Or maybe I was Sue deprived. Or horse deprived. I craved all three — sun, Sue, and my own goddamn horse. If I were riding Aunt Jemima, I'd discuss it with her and she would advise me. Alan, she'd say, just tend to the task at hand and the rest will follow. No matter what the situation, she had a way of setting things right with the world. I set my mind on her for the rest of the ride home.

Aunt Jemima had been a handful to train. As a young colt, this little grulla-colored mare didn't like what we were trying to teach her and was slow to offer her trust. Her older sister Tequila, a big, strong, willing cow horse, held a special spot in my string of horses

2. Aunt Jemima

at Lazy B. I was willing to put up with Aunt Jemima's crankiness because of how much I enjoyed riding her sister. When Jemima got big enough to ride, I assigned her to Rodney, one of the ranch hands, to break. He had a way with young horses. But he had one fault: he liked to ride bucking horses. With her peppery temper, Aunt Jemima would buck if challenged, and Rodney seemed to be constantly challenging her.

I'd watch the two of them go at it in the corral. "Why do you try to make that mare buck?" I'd say to Rodney. "You're supposed to be breaking her to be gentle. If you keep making her buck, she'll learn how to buck harder and harder and then she won't be good for anything."

"Aw, I'm just having fun with her. She can't buck hard enough to scare anyone," he'd reply.

I finally got so annoyed with Rodney's attitude that I took over riding Aunt Jemima. She was still young, and compared to the four or five horses in my string, much smaller. I saddled her up a couple times and rode her around the headquarters corrals. When she tried to buck me off, I pulled her head up and scolded her. "Jemima, we're not out here to put on a rodeo. We're here to work cattle, so get your head up and let's do our job." She understood me. It didn't take long for the bucking to stop.

I had been on her only twice when I decided to take her out on the range to do what normally would be an easy job. We needed to move a herd of steers to a pasture I recently had leased at the Bilbo Ranch about fifty-five miles away. Due to distance, the moving would be done by truck. The cattle had long been gentled and we just needed to unload them and get them acclimated to the ranch. Aunt Jemima was still a green broke, if that, so the day's activity would be good experience for her. If it had been a bigger job, I would have opted to ride Saber, my number-one horse that easily could do every job that needed to be done horseback.

It took two hours to haul our heavy load to the east side of Lordsburg, New Mexico. The crew of five cowboys and I drove the two trailers into open pasture. A forty-foot, single-deck trailer divided into three compartments held the cattle. With a roof made of pipes, it had provided an open-aired excursion for the fifty head of steers. Our horses stood in a much smaller trailer that we unloaded as soon as we parked. Though it wasn't quite noon, the early summer air felt warm and dry. A thin layer of dust seemed to cover everything.

As I re-cinched Aunt Jemima's saddle, I previewed the day with her.

"Jemima, here's what we're going to do. First, we're going to unload those cattle. They'll come trotting off the trailer and when they see us they'll stop. So I need you to help hold them. Once they're in a nice bunch, we'll drive them to the water trough by the holding tank so they know where to get a drink. They'll start walking around and grazing. We'll make sure they're comfortable before we head back home. All you have to do is keep your eye on the cattle and we'll do just fine." I rubbed her neck. I got the feeling she understood me.

I climbed aboard and joined four cowboys already on horseback. We formed a semicircle at the back of the trailer to act as a net to prevent the steers from spreading. I could feel Aunt Jemima's anticipation. She was like a seventh grader getting ready for her first full-court basketball game in the school gym.

The remaining man, the gate opener, was on foot. The springs of the trailer squeaked as the cattle began shifting and impatient bawls filled the air. He swung the back gates open and stepped out of the way as the first steers burst out like they were running from a bomb about to explode. They didn't stop once they hit dirt. There was no mistaking they were spooked. The cowboys and I gave ground, trying to stay ahead of them. But there they came at a high run, with the next group right behind them, and the third group right behind them. Within minutes they had broken through our net and were stampeding in every direction, feeding panic to the herd. No one had a chance to think what could have possibly frightened them. The cowboys had spurred their horses into a full gallop. Jemima seemed to know what to do and was in the right place.

We turned our horses, yelling to each other or using hand signals to communicate over the thunder of pounding hooves.

"I've got these over here."

"Get 'em in one group. We'll bend 'em round and take them back."

"Stay ahead of them if you can, boys."

Everyone's adrenaline cranked—cowboy, cattle, and horse. This was exactly the situation in which you wanted to be on a horse like Saber. Here I was on this little bitty horse that had barely been ridden. Instead of running her first full-court press in the school gym, Aunt Jemima had been tossed right into the heart of an NBA game. But there we were, galloping and turning and trying to ring-in steers rippling away from us. Aunt Jemima was fully engaged. It was as if she had a sneak preview at the playbook. I was asking her to do what I would have asked Saber to do. She was rising to the occasion and making a hand.

For an hour we labored to turn those steers sideways, slow them down to a trot, drive them into a bunch, and bend them back near the water trough. Every one of us galloped several miles to get the job done. The backs and armpits of the crew's shirts were drenched in sweat and sweat dripped down the horses' flanks and necks. Only one renegade steer wouldn't stop. Aunt Jemima and I watched him jump over a fence into the neighbor's pasture. I could feel her pulling me to go after him. She knew where he was supposed to be and it wasn't over there. Her work was not yet done.

I tried to calm her down. "Jemima, he's too far ahead of us to ever catch him. And you'll run yourself down if I let you go after him."

She didn't like that answer. She kept her head up and watched him grow smaller. She was telling me she was good for the chase. I could feel that she still had energy. It was my job to figure out how much and not let her overrun. I know the feeling of wanting to do the job right and get it done. She had just proven to me that she was a game player. I needed to honor her request.

I relented. "Okay, let's see if we can find a gate."

I turned her and she went into an easy gallop along the fence. A gate appeared and I got off, opened it, and remounted.

The steer looked to be about a mile away.

"If you think you can catch him, I'm going to pitch you the slack. You pick the pace, Jemima. Take it kind of easy, though, because we have a long way to go." I hoped she heard my cheers more than my doubts.

She leapt forward without a spur and the chase was on. She chose an easy, steady gallop. The distance between the steer and us began to decrease. Her endurance and strength amazed me. We were covering country, past mesquite and creosote bush. Pretty soon,

I heard a second set of hooves hitting the ground and smelled the disturbed dust rising up into the warm air. The gap between the steer and us closed to one hundred yards. My doubts dissipated. By golly, she just might catch this guy.

The steer jumped off a small bank into a sandy canyon. Without hesitation, Jemima followed.

"Aunt Jemima, if you can catch him, I'll rope him."

I took my rope and built a loop. Jemima's gait suddenly changed from smooth to choppy and right then, I knew she had nothing left. She had hit the anaerobic wall. The steer was twenty feet in front of us. I started swinging the loop around my head, aimed for the steer's horns, and threw it. It floated through the air and settled over the exhausted animal's head. I yanked the slack and dallied the rope around the saddle horn. Everything came to a complete halt. We couldn't have gone another two feet. Between Aunt Jemima and the steer panting and my heart pounding, I couldn't hear the cicadas buzz.

We sat there and waited for the cowboys to show up. They weren't far behind.

"You take this steer," I said, handing the rope to one of them. "I've gotta take care of my horse."

I dismounted and stood there, wiping sweat from Aunt Jemima's neck and shoulders. She stood there, legs splayed, sides heaving. I continued to rub and love on her until her panting slowed.

"Jemima, you gave me one hundred percent of who you are. You got the job done, baby. You have the biggest heart I've ever seen," I kept telling her. "You've made me a friend for life." After she recovered, I slowly rode her back to the trailer.

I had arrived in that pasture anticipating the ordinary but left having experienced the extraordinary. It wasn't the stampede that was unique, or lassoing the steer. Responding to the thrill and tension and adventure of the unexpected is all part of being a cowboy. It defines who you are. What I found extraordinary was the heart of the horse I rode, the effort she gave, an effort few horses ever give. It was an amazing day, the day I fell in love with Aunt Jemima.

I still loved her to pieces. Maybe I could ship her up to South Dakota after things got settled. I bet she'd relish it up here. In the meantime, maybe John could find me a horse of my own.

Neither Congress nor the Bureau of Indian Affairs had given us the green light of approval for the sanctuary. I couldn't call Congress, but I could call Roger Running Horse. "My supervisor told me she's been so busy that she just hasn't had time to address your issues. I'll press her a little harder this week. I'm sure she'll approve it right away once she sees it." I tamped down my frustration, said I would check in again, and turned my attention to the ranch's needs.

John and I got busy spreading phosphorous on one-third of the hay meadow. If the results turned out to be as good as I hoped, we'd do another section the following year. The soil content within individual pastures varied, an invitation for horses to overgraze the tastier grass and ignore the rest, so we reconfigured the fence lines to create pastures with as much common soil as possible.

I put the word out around the community that I was looking for some day laborers—a painter for the buildings at headquarters and some hands to start tearing down the sheep barn. John was right. There were more jobs than local workers. I ended up recruiting a painter I knew from Tucson, who also happened to be an alcoholic, but he did good work when sober, which was what he would be if sequestered on the Arnold Ranch. He said okay, he'd dry out for a while, so I flew him up to South Dakota and set him up with a sprayer, fifty gallons of paint, and a case of ginger ale. Two weeks later, he was a new person and so was headquarters. Just looking at the bright-red barn and the white house with green trim made me puff up like a rooster. I returned him to Arizona, then flew in two brothers who had worked on Lazy B, Carlos and Ramon, to tear down the sheep barn. They had hauled half the salvage wood to headquarters when the first of three political apples dropped in the bucket.

Senator DeConcini's aide bubbled the news over the phone. The senator had created a rider granting the BLM authority to contract for a wild horse sanctuary, then recruited enough support to tack it onto a bill that sailed through Congress. This was the linchpin of the sanctuary, the authorization we had been waiting for. It was like we crested the ridge, caught sight of the finish line, and starting rolling down the hill. Goddamn, the sanctuary was going to happen. It felt exciting, intimidating, and vindicating. My feet hadn't even touched the ground before the second apple fell. Within the week, a BLM rep called from Washington DC. Though far less effusive than the aide, he said the bureau was on board but to hold on to my hat, we had details to work out.

Dayton and I drove up to the BLM office in Rapid City five different times to haggle over those details. The final version of the contract called for us to keep all mustangs we received in good flesh and good health. We were to turn them out on grass as much as possible and, when necessary during the winter, feed them hay. We were granted the power to euthanize sick and injured animals. Each month we were to submit a statement that accounted for each horse, and each month the State of South Dakota would receive payment from the BLM and apportion it to us. I would receive $1.15 per horse per day and Dayton a tad more since his smaller operation was less efficient than our larger acreage. The contract would extend for four years. And the final detail: the BLM agreed to ship three hundred wild horses to Dayton's ranch and fifteen hundred horses to the Arnold Ranch. Yes, one thousand five hundred unadoptable wild mustangs would take up residence on the ranch I had purchased on a whim. The vision that had been thrust before me was being brought to life bearing my blood and sweat. If you can have an out-of-body experience signing on a dotted line, I did.

But one detail remained. That third apple had yet to fall. "How about if I set up a meeting with your supervisor?" I said over the phone to Roger Running Horse. He said good idea, especially in light of getting horses soon. Congratulations. How exciting. Blah, blah, blah. He would get on this so as not to delay delivery of the horses.

Nothing happened.

I called again. "What the hell is going on?" I didn't bother to hide my anger. The smiling snake charmer gave me some lamebrain excuse about an urgent situation the supervisor had to attend to. I hung up totally frustrated.

I could feel panic start to rise. This bureaucratic beast had its jaws wide open, ready to swallow our project. I began to quiz neighbors and consider every possible angle. Do you think we can just go ahead and turn the horses out? Will the BIA fine us if they find horses running on their land? Will they hire cowboys to round them up and take them away? Where would they take so many horses? I decided there was a fly in the ointment somewhere, and one way or another I would have a face-to-face with this supervisor.

I got in the pickup and set out for Pine Ridge prepared to go on strike and raise hell until I met the supervisor. On an impulse, I stopped at Stan Whipple's office in St. Francis. When I told him where I was headed and why, he broke out in a big grin and told me to sit down. He handed me a cup of coffee.

"Your nemesis is gone," he said. I assumed he was talking about the supervisor. "No, no. Roger Running Horse. He was your worst enemy. Did his utmost to completely block your project. He was transferred out of state to another job." Stan explained that he and the other employees of the tribe had watched Running Horse weave his treachery but felt their hands were tied. They didn't want to make the war with the BIA any worse. "I'm sorry, man. We

3. Entrance to Mustang Meadows Ranch

watched him manipulate you, and we couldn't do anything about it." This was my first, though not my last, exposure to interagency chicanery. Running Horse never submitted any of our plans to his supervisor and even went so far as to ask the tribe to not approve our request. He was one bad dude.

A few days later, I presented the sanctuary plans to the supervisor. She gave immediate approval to graze the horses on BIA land. The last golden apple dropped in the bucket. I drove back to the ranch in a euphoric cloud. I passed the gnarled post. Just before the cattle guard, I stopped, put the truck in park, crossed my arms over the steering wheel, and looked out over the prairie. I tried to imagine mustangs galloping across the hills, ears back, tails outstretched. Having lived my life with horses, I thought it would be easy, yet I couldn't quite conjure the image. Would they be happy, aloof, crazy? Would they sound like thunder? Would I be right there, riding close to them? Soon enough I'd find out. I put the truck in drive and crossed over onto the ranch.

That's when the ranch spoke up. No longer would it be called the old Arnold Ranch. Nor would it be called the Day Ranch. It was begging for its own identity, and what it wanted was Mustang Meadows Ranch.

"I like it," I said out loud.

Mustang Meadows Ranch, the first government-sponsored wild horse sanctuary in the United States.

PART TWO

CHAPTER SEVEN

A Stubborn Start

It was mid-September and I was puttering in my office, accomplishing about as much as an expectant father back in the days when we were relegated to rank vending machine coffee and curled magazines in maternity waiting rooms. Yesterday's phone call had unleashed waves of that same nervous energy. The voice at the other end said a load of horses was ready to ship out from Bloomfield, Nebraska, and would show up around noon tomorrow. Meaning today. Meaning in two hours. Meaning I had better find something else to ease the jitters.

I shoved the bookkeeping ledger in the desk drawer and grabbed my hat. A chat with Clyde, that's what I needed. Earlier I had sent John and Russ out to the West Whitelands pasture to repair a windmill. No sense in having everyone wait around headquarters. They would be back before the horses arrived. The Pitkin kids had tried to talk their way out of going to school, but John reassured them that unloading the horses was no big deal. The mustangs would run down the truck ramp into the corral in minutes. "Besides," he said, "they'll be with us for a long time." But a shadowed rendition of their collective pout crossed his face when I doled out the windmill assignment.

The intermittent whir of a distant drill pulled me toward the corrals. In one of the small corrals north of the barn Carlos straddled the top rung of metal tubing, steadying one end of a long piece of lumber while Ramon attached the other end to a post with lag screws. I opened the main gate into the large training arena. At dawn John and I had walked through it for the fiftieth time, shaking the fencing and rub boards that Carlos and Ramon had reinforced. It was a fortress. Strong enough to withstand the power of angry or crazed mustangs and, at six feet tall, too high for them to jump.

I walked across the arena into the cool sanctuary of the barn and let my eyes adjust. Dust lazed in the shafts of light. The calming scent of worn leather, seasoned wood, horse feed, and horse soothed my nerves. From his stall, my new horse, Clyde, gave a nicker of recognition. We had gotten acquainted over the last several months after John bought him for me. A handsome sorrel, Clyde fit the bill as a good ranch horse. He wasn't flashy or high-strung but a solid horse to ride. I grabbed the curry brush off the wooden box next to the grain barrel.

"Hey buddy," I said, walking into the stall. I stroked his nose with my hand. "How ya doin'?" I ran the brush along one side of his neck. His coat had started to thicken, a response to the expanding chill of nights and decreasing warmth of days. He pushed against the pressure, his head arcing one way, then another in a figure eight of contentment.

"It's a big day. Our new life is going to begin." The muscles of his shoulders shifted under my hands as he stretched his head forward. "I have to tell you — and this stays between you and me — we have it all to learn with the wild horses." I stroked down the withers to his front leg, my free hand following the wake of the brush, a comforting motion for both of us. "Jesus, fifteen hundred of them," I said. Clyde gave his head a little shake and snorted. "What if we can't handle them? What if they refuse our training? Refuse to be our friends?" I could hear Red and Roy insisting that a herd of horses couldn't be trained and would never accept friendship. Clyde reached around to the brush and nuzzled my stalled hand. "Well, I can't help it. You've gotta admit, it's a little frightening."

I moved up to the swale of his back, home to my saddle. The brush bumped over a clump of hair wadded by sweat. I smoothed it out and felt carefully for tiny thorns that might rub into his skin and create a sore.

"Well, it's too late to back out now. The fat's in the fire." I rounded up my fears, stashed them on a shelf in the back of my mind, and tuned in to every cell and fiber saying the sanctuary would be a success. The ranch was a horse's paradise, like an all-inclusive resort with an endless supply of grass and open pasture. On these grounds no one would chase, harass, or kidnap. Our job was to replace the horses' mistrust with trust, their fear with friendship, and I believed we would succeed.

"I'm telling you, Clyde, it's all in the training." Clyde swished his tail and pawed a front hoof. I pulled the brush along his back hip and felt him tense. His head came to attention and he wiggled one ear. I stopped. Only the screeching drill and sharp caw of a crow reached my ears.

"All right now, what would you think about getting some fresh air?" Clyde pushed his nose toward the barn wall. That's when I heard it. The distant rumble of a diesel engine. A vehicle had to be within two miles of ranch headquarters for a motor to be heard, at least by a human. Judging by its throaty growl, the vehicle was large. For a moment I thought maybe I had lost track of time, that amid my musings, morning had shifted into afternoon, but the slant of sunlight slipping through the barn door said high noon had not arrived.

It had to be the horses.

"Damn, they're early." So much for John and Russ being present. At this point, there was no way to summon them. I'd have to manage alone. I gave Clyde a pat, returned the brush, and set out to greet the driver. I was halfway across the lawn when the cab of a semi edged into view and behind it a trailer as long as five flatbed pickups. The beast ground to a stop where the road forked.

4. The first truckload of horses arrives

The driver rolled down the window and tipped up the bill of his ball cap. "You Alan Day?"

"Yes, sir," I said. The air held an astringent, wild smell. "You sure got on the road early."

"Yep, we started loading these guys at four-thirty this morning. Went without a hitch. Gives me time to head back to load cattle for points north." He patted the steering wheel as if satisfied with the day so far. "Horses got a bit of a ride over that road of yours, though."

"Yeah, well. Be glad you weren't here last week before we filled in a dozen giant potholes. You'd be cussing me up and down right now." A horse whinnied inside the trailer. The cargo was eager to unload. "Follow the road around to the left and I'll open the gate for you." I hopped on the running board and grabbed onto the mirror bracket. The driver shifted the rig into low gear and along the road we rolled, past the training arena to the north corral. I opened the gate and he made a U-turn and backed up to the chute as I spotted him. By the third try, it was a perfect fit. The airbrakes hissed and the engine breathed a sigh, then stopped. Carlos and Ramon had abandoned their work and sauntered over to watch the festivities. Debbie stood next to them loading film in her camera.

The driver climbed down. From a cubbyhole on the side of the cab, he removed rubber boots, coveralls, and gloves, his uniform for working with livestock, and put them on. He walked around to the back of the truck and looked at me: "You ready?"

My voice said yes, my thoughts said I hope so. The driver walked up the chute to the back of the trailer and unlatched and pushed up the gate. He quickly climbed out of the way. A bay head with a white star between the eyes popped out into the sunlight, ears forward, eyes inquisitive. Debbie's camera clicked. The bay headed down the chute. On his tail came a sleek brown mustang, shaggy mane bouncing in the breeze. Black, white, gray, a palomino, and more browns—in less than two minutes a baker's dozen had entered the corral. They shook their heads and snorted. A few trotted around exercising the stiffness out of their legs.

Before any of us bystanders could comment, the driver opened the gate for the next bunch of thirteen to exit. Down they came, single file, as easily as the first. Although these horses were a far cry from the thoroughbreds of a white-fenced Kentucky ranch, they also weren't nearly as skittish as the horses that I had watched in Palomino Valley. Their Bloomfield experience had taught them not to panic at the sight of humans. Their frames were filled out like they had been eating regular meals and their coats had a healthy sheen.

The driver's footsteps echoed along the metal bottom of the trailer. We heard the third gate open. He jogged out, climbed over the chute, and jumped with a thud to the ground. Debbie put her camera to her eye. Nothing happened. No clopping footsteps. No heads poking out. I squinted down the shadowed lane of trailer.

5. The first wild mustangs to unload

At the far end, I could make out seven or eight horse rumps in an arc, heads down in a defensive huddle.

The driver reached under the seat of his cab and pulled out a billy club. He banged it on the side of the truck. "Come on, now. Git." Metal rattled and echoed inside the trailer. The horses held their position. He continued banging, but no movement ensued. "Well I'll be damned. They got in there just fine. Why won't they come out?"

I turned to Carlos and Ramon. "You two go over to the other side of the truck and start pounding. Debbie, you come on this side."

The five of us pounded and shouted and pounded some more. I expected the lead horse to turn at any moment and exit the trailer. But it didn't. Two or three minutes of noisemaking failed to dissolve the invisible bonds that held the bunch together.

I grabbed a stick from the ground and pushed it through a slat of the trailer. It ran into the muscled side of a horse. "Move," I yelled, to no avail.

Carlos climbed on top of the trailer. Ramon followed. They

pounded and yelled. "*Vaya, stupido caballo.*" I peered through the slats but didn't see any movement inside. Debbie looked at me, eyebrows raised in question. I was mystified. What had scared them?

"I've got some hot shots in the back of the cab we could use," said the driver.

Good Lord, the horses had been here all of fifteen minutes and already I was being asked to break one of my top rules. Some ranchers and haulers of livestock resort to the electric prods to get cattle moving. The animals get a pretty good sting, as I discovered once when I tested one on myself. I considered them inhumane. There had to be another way. If John was here we would be able to noodle over some ideas, but I was solo on this one.

"Want me to get them out?" The driver had his hand on the cab door.

"No," I said. "We don't use prod poles."

"Okay, do what you want, but get these sonofabitches off. I've got to get back on the road. That next load is waiting."

Debbie, Carlos, and Ramon looked at me, the boss, the supposed horse expert. The sun had reached full strength and a dribble of sweat ran down my back. Shit, shit, shit. I never had a horse that wouldn't come out of a trailer. My first contact with wild horses, and I'm poking a stick into them and don't know what the hell to do next. I wanted to yank them out. Yeah, like I would really yank out the remaining fourteen horses. Maybe pull them out, but not yank.

Pull. Now there was an idea.

The image of a truck stuck in a desert wash roaring with summer rains flashed through my mind. The Lazy B cowboys and I had been struggling to free it. I was fourteen and didn't want to meet my dad's eyes if we came home without one of our vehicles. As a last-ditch effort, I suggested tying one end of some nylon rope to the Jeep on dry land and the other end to the truck stuck tire-deep in water. The rope stretched to breaking point, but it held and pulled the truck up the bank.

"You guys wait here a minute. I have an idea." I headed for the barn.

I grabbed three saddle ropes from the tack room, knotted them together, and coiled the long rope. On my way out, I grabbed a broom. The tractor we had been using to haul lumber sat parked on the side of the shed. I slung the looped rope over my shoulder, climbed up in the tractor seat, and balancing the broom on my lap, drove along the outside of the corrals to the gate. Carlos ran up and opened it. The horses in the corral scattered nervously out of the way. I swung the tractor around and backed it up to the bottom of the chute. I tied one end of the rope to the tractor's back hitch.

"Carlos, *aqui*," I said, pointing to the tractor seat. Carlos got up onto the tractor. "When I give the go-ahead," I explained in Spanish, "you take off. Keep it strong and steady. I'll tell you when to stop. You'll have to back up quickly to release the tension in the rope. It'll be less than a minute. Make sure you stop right when I say." With rope and broom in hand, I went up the chute and cautiously approached the knot of horses. Tails swished.

"Okay, guys, we're going to have a little dance here," I said while making a loop with the rope. "This is your new home and you're going to like it. Trust me on this." I took a few slow steps along the side of the trailer, closer to the bunch. If the group bolted, I wanted to be out of the way. "But you won't know that unless you give it a try. So I'm here to help you get your feet going in the right direction." I slid the loop over the end of the broom.

"Who's up first for this adventure? You can tell the others out there all about it. How you got pulled off the trailer and into the corral in less than sixty seconds." The bunch twitched and shuffled and warned me away with snorts. Every head remained down.

"It's getting kind of warm in here. The fresh air and breeze is going to feel good. And all that hay, it's real sweet. You can stretch your legs, too."

As if curious to see if there really was a brightly lit world, a horse close to me lifted its head. I swung the broom handle through the air, dropped the loop over its head, and tightened it.

"GO!" I shouted out the trailer. Carlos hit the accelerator. The rope stretched tight around the horse's neck. The startled animal spun around toward the chute. Down it went on its rump, forelegs stuck out trying to resist the drag. Its hooves clamored and tapped against the slippery metal floor. The rope pulled. The horse flailed against the lack of oxygen. A few more feet and he was in the chute. I signaled to Carlos to keep pulling. The horse's eyes bugged and he was gasping. He slid to the bottom and I ran down the incline.

"Whoa, Carlos!" Tractor and horse stopped. Carlos shifted into reverse to give the rope slack. I loosened the noose and pulled it over the horse's head. He scrambled to his feet shaking his head, sides heaving. He gave me a good glare before trotting off to join his compatriots.

Ramon and Debbie clapped, but there was no reason to take a bow. Thirteen horses stood in the truck behind me. Three hundred sixty-four days and twenty-three hours of year one with the horses stood in front of me. The driver checked his watch.

I waved Carlos back into position, slid the loop on the broom handle, renewed my determination, and walked back into the truck. Horses jostled.

"That wasn't so bad, was it? A quick dance. Who wants to go next?" A roan raised its head. I swung the broom handle over her like a boom on a movie set, raised the handle, and let the loop slide off. Bingo. I yelled to Carlos. Panic filled the animal's eyes and limbs. But it was a quick ride to the chute and down it. Again, the rope loosened easily under my hands. I made sure that it would not become a deadly noose. The roan took a few deep gasps and clopped into the corral.

Carlos and I became more efficient. Each time I approached, the horses stood quieter. I chatted and they responded by looking up. I was looping the broom for the tenth time when a pretty chestnut horse with a long black mane turned on her own and trotted the length of the trailer and right down the chute. She pulled the other horses with her single file like they had practiced the drill a hundred times. The gallery erupted into another round of applause.

Maybe these last five decided they didn't want to endure the brief struggle like their buddies had. Maybe they finally smelled the hay. Maybe they realized they were here to stay and no sense fighting it. Maybe they were weary of hearing me talk. I shrugged my shoulders. It was not for us to know.

Before the driver latched the doors of the trailer, John and Russ pulled up in the pickup. They eyed the tractor in the corral, the knotted saddle rope snaking behind it.

"So how'd it go?" John asked. He knew damn well how it went.

"Went just fine. These five horses here," I said, pointing, "just walked off without a hitch." And thankfully without rope burns.

The only one burned so far was me. Fortunately it wasn't a first-degree burn or even a third-degree burn. It was more like feeling singed around the edges. With thirty-five more truckloads of mustangs expected, I just prayed I wouldn't go up in flames.

CHAPTER EIGHT

Vying for the Upper Hand

I saddled Clyde and, like every morning for the past four weeks, we headed through the corrals to the horse pasture just north of headquarters. Four hundred horses now lived there. Semitrailers had chugged up the ranch road two or three times a week, bringing more horses from Bloomfield. Later, after that facility emptied, they would come from Nevada, New Mexico, and sometimes Wyoming. The anticipation of horses arriving drifted over fence lines and pulled in neighbors and an occasional local journalist, all armed with cameras. On days we had an audience, the cowboys and I would stand a little taller or sit straighter in our saddles. Thankfully we never again had to deal with balky horses that refused to unload. But the mustangs made sure to show their resistance in other ways.

I dismounted and opened the gate. The horses closest to me shot up their heads and flipped back their ears as if responding to the entrance of a drill sergeant. Hooves thumped the sand and snorts filled the air, encoded messages alerting the others to come to attention. But instead of lining up for inspection, the herd turned in unison and hauled ass in the other direction, away from the enemy. Me. Their caretaker. By the time I shut the gate and swung back in the saddle, they had disappeared over hill and dale, headed for the farthest corner of the square-mile pasture.

This wasn't the first time we had gone through this drill. During their first week at the ranch, they remained in the corrals.

As long as no one disturbed them, they stayed calm. If they felt threatened, they bunched together in a corner, heads down. At week's end, we turned them out to the horse pasture. They had yet to learn that we came waving an olive branch, not hot shots or long sticks with white flags.

Clyde trotted through the open space, unperturbed by the scent of his unruly wild cousins.

"Let's hold up here," I said.

We stopped on the brow of the first hill. The herd had vanished. I hopped off and dropped the reins, ground-tying Clyde. He didn't waste time burrowing his nose in the grass. I swished my boot through the plants. Less resistance than a few days ago. I dropped to my hands and knees, the sandy loam yielding to my weight in a way the hard sands of Arizona never did. I examined the soil, searching for gaps where plants had been yanked from the ground by the teeth of hungry horses. If cows had been in this pasture, their bovine jaws would have sculpted the vegetation into neat teepees. Horses dive straight down like bomber pilots, mouths open, and bite, giving grass a flat top haircut or uprooting young plants.

Clyde and I rode to another section of the pasture, then to another and another. A few times, we saw horses in the distance grazing. They were grazing well, all right, maybe too well. The grass had shrunk by about 50 percent and its density had thinned. The pasture needed a rest, which meant the horses needed to move to fresh prairie. I knew this time would come. I had hoped it would be after the horses were trained, but if I waited to complete their training, this pasture would be trashed. Within less than half a year of owning the ranch, I would have broken my promise to the land.

Tomorrow was Saturday. Maybe Jordan could recruit some of his buddies to help move the horses. A little voice inside me said the more the merrier. At least I thought the word was merrier. In retrospect, it might have been something more like warier.

"Tomorrow we may have a helluva race," I said to Clyde. "Get ready for some real cowboying."

Seven of us were horseback—me, John, Russ, and Marty Blocker, a longtime cowboy who was so enamored with the wild horses that he had been volunteering his help on weekends since they had arrived, plus Jordan and a couple of his high school buddies, Mike and Jason. On Lazy B, this size crew could round up a thousand head of cattle on twenty square miles. Even though we had one-twentieth the space, I welcomed the extra hands. A chilly easterly wind had kicked up during the night. We gathered in the corral, collars up and hands gloved, to go through tactical maneuvers.

"The minute we get to the gate, the horses are going to bolt," I said. "They usually take off for the back northwest corner. Let's head out there in a line, run them round the outside of the pasture, then get in position to wing them through the gate." In such a small pasture, this was the only plan possible.

"Piece of cake," said Jason. The cocky teen crowd seconded him. If the horses had been trained, I might have echoed that second, but my silent vote went to the more conservative "wait- and-see" side.

The herd was grazing about a quarter mile from the gate in a valley between hills. Our appearance tripped an electric current that zinged through the bunch. Within moments the horses were on the move, heading up and over the opposite hill.

"Dang, those suckers are fast," said Jason, sounding a bit more humbled.

The last group of mares galloped out of sight. A curtain of dust rose from the far side of the hill, separating our team from theirs. I glanced at Russ, Marty, and John. They wore that look a seasoned cowboy gets when faced with a challenge. Every species has its silent language and *Cowboy sapiens* is no different. They sat straight in their saddles, one arm bent at a right angle holding the reins, squinting out from under their hats, assessing the situation.

We all knew the mustangs could run faster than the wind pushing against our backs. Our horses could run too, but they carried a rider and a saddle. We'd have to be the smarter players on this field.

We set out at a trot to put our rudimentary game plan into action. Russ, Marty, and Jason peeled into a line on my right; John, Jordan, and Mike spread out on my left. We stretched several hundred yards. We swung in formation toward the west corner of the pasture just to make sure no horses had wandered over there. Finding none, we turned northwest.

Four hundred horses clumped in the corner, facing this way and that. We closed in at a slow, nonthreatening pace. They began to vibrate with panic. Heads shook and bobbed, tails twitched. Nervous whinnies sifted through the wind. Stranger danger. Get ready to run. We had trespassed ten yards into their personal space when a group of lead horses bolted out of the bunch at a full gallop. Along the north fence they raced, like pent-up steam escaping a boiler, heading east away from us. The herd fell into a stampede maybe fifty horses wide and rocketed toward the northeast corner of the pasture. I expected them to stop there, but instead they turned the corner and kept going south, picking up speed. At that speed they would beat us to the south corner. I waved my arm in the air, signaling the crew to my right to change directions. If we crossed the pasture as the crow flies, maybe we could get to the gate first. Unfortunately, the gate wasn't in the corner, but about a hundred yards beyond it. We'd have to arc our line from behind the gate out into the pasture. The horses would see seven cowboys blocking their way and slow down. That's when we would wing them through the gate and into the corral. We galloped parallel to the dust cloud rising behind the hills on our left. But when we bounded over the final hill, the horses were ahead of us.

"They're about to round the corner already," yelled Marty, and he spurred his horse into high gear to try to get in position to turn them into the gate. John was close behind.

The lead mares took the last corner like race cars at the Indianapolis 500 headed for the finish line. Marty and John were still several hundred yards short of being in position. The horses roared past the gate without so much as a glance. If there had been a checkered flag, it would have swished down declaring the mustangs the winners.

I pulled up and watched four hundred crazed horses run past me, necks outstretched, blindly following each other, intent on doing a victory lap in full throttle. The wind pushed gritty air into my face, my nose, my ears. From somewhere, a little voice taunted. "You think you can train these horses? Who's the sucker now?" I hit the mute button. That's the last thing I needed to hear. As it was, the horses had written the first chapter in the training manual. It was titled "How to Get Your Way."

I edged Clyde out of the dust storm and the cowboys followed. Twelve eyes looked at me. "Well, boys, we lost that one," I said. "Score is horses ten, us zero."

"More like twenty to zero," said Marty and turned his head to spit. Defeat always stings more when you're on a fast horse.

My mind sifted through the slim pickings of game plans. "We're going to play the second half a little differently. Russ and Jordan, you go roust those bastards out of the corner and swing in behind them. Follow them on around. The rest of us will spread out and be ready to turn them in the gate. Everyone got it?" Heads shook in acknowledgment. Russ and Jordan galloped off and the rest of us took our positions. "Mike, move over toward John. There's too big a gap." I waved him to the left. A horse would accept that space as an invitation to bolt through it.

This plan had to work. Sweet Jesus, we couldn't be having horse races every time we tried to move the herd. The other grazing pastures were six to eight square miles. If we had to keep repeating this gathering game, it would be chaos. Our horses would tire by the second go-around and the crew would get frustrated.

Today wasn't so bad; it was our first attempt and felt more like adventure than anything else. Training. That's what these horses needed. Would their wild spirits respond? I kicked the worry aside and focused on the distant cloud of dust inching toward us along the fence line.

The lead horses galloped into sight. They looked to be going a step or two slower. No wonder. They had been running almost nonstop for about four miles. The lead horses blew around the corner, saw us, slowed down, and realized that this time they had no other choice. They turned and went through the gate without a hitch.

"Those bastards knew where the gate was all along," said Marty. "They were just testing us."

I had to agree with him. They had entered this pasture through that gate. They knew where it was. They were letting us know they would take the gate when they chose and not a lap sooner. We were on the scoreboard, but the horses had won the match.

The roundup pointed in bold letters to the need for training. They were only responding in the way in which they had been taught: Humans are the enemy. Flee from them. We needed to change their thinking. More than anything, I wanted to succeed in doing that. In the past I successfully trained horses, but I also had failures, and I did not want to relive the pain of failure, especially as I had experienced it a decade ago.

I had been managing Lazy B full-time for about eight years and had just lost a horse from my string, so I needed a replacement. I spent quite a little time observing our crop of young horses and chose a good-looking filly whose mama I had ridden years back, before we turned her out with the mares to raise foals. She had been a nice horse, very solid and good to ride. Like her mother, this filly was blond, with broad shoulders, a large frame, and an amiable disposition, all traits of a good horse. I decided to name her Candy after one of our family's friends, whose sunny disposition and pretty face always made me smile.

Our longtime cowboy Claude Tippets heard me calling the newest horse in our remuda Candy. He said, "Alan, that's a really bad name for that horse."

"What makes you say that?" I said. "Didn't know a bad name made a bad horse."

"It's too pretty a name. That filly can't carry a name like that and carry you at the same time. She'll die."

Maybe Claude was losing it. Next he'd be telling me to keep salt in my chaps to throw over my shoulder. I shrugged. "Well, we'll see about that."

"Nope, she won't live. Ya named her wrong," he insisted. "She should be called Squaw Piss."

If I had seen a crystal ball sitting on the corral post maybe I would have changed her name, even to Squaw Piss, but I didn't, so she remained Candy, and Candy remained sweet with one exception. When I went to fetch her in the horse pasture, she'd nuzzle me and enjoy being petted. She remained cheerful while being saddled, but as soon as I'd get on her, she'd put her head down and go to bucking. She couldn't buck very hard, so she never bucked me off, but when the cycle started, I had a hard time getting her to stop. I figured she was one of those young horses that had to go through the bucking phase. Eventually I'd just ride her out of it, so I kept riding her in an effort to do that.

She still hadn't ditched her habit the day I saddled her for a pleasure ride. The summer rains had spit-shined the ranch and persuaded grass to grow, especially in the big floodwater draw that ran past headquarters in the east pasture. An inviting blanket of green covered its normally dry dirt bottom. About a mile and half down, the draw spread out into a big hole, maybe a hundred yards long and fifty yards wide, that remained bone dry until the summer rains filled it. Then it turned into a twelve-foot-deep water hole. I thought we'd go check it out, then ride through the pasture.

We hadn't even left the corral yet when Candy went to bucking. When I got on her she bucked. When we went out the gates she bucked. When we rode through the draw she bucked. Each time, she'd buck a few jumps, and I'd get her pulled up and scold her either verbally or with a little bit of corporal punishment—a spur, a slap of the reins—enough to let her know she was misbehaving. This went on and on as we progressed down the draw. I thought she'd get her head up and start paying attention to the work we were doing, which was nothing more than me riding her trying to enjoy the scenery. But no. She had to buck.

By the time we arrived at the water hole, we were hot and downright irritated with each other. The waterline had edged up as far as it could go without spilling onto the land. The calm water invited us to cool our tempers and wash the sweat off. I decided we would go for a swim. Since a horse can't buck in water, at least that nonsense would end for a bit. I rode Candy to the edge of the water, but she refused to put her feet in. I spurred her. She turned left. I turned her back and spurred her again. She turned right. That darn horse was doing everything possible to avoid the water. This was ridiculous. I grabbed the get-down rope with its big cotton knot at the end, swung it with one hand, and popped her a good one on the hip.

I should have named her Pegasus, because Candy just about sprouted wings. She leapt into the air and plunged in the middle of the water. I slid off the saddle still holding the reins, prepared to do what cowboys do when you swim with a horse. With one hand, you hold either the saddle horn or the tail and let the horse pull you around. Kind of a western version of swimming with a dolphin, though I wouldn't exactly call twenty pound chaps and a pair of pointed leather boots a version of a wetsuit.

I didn't get a chance to grab the saddle horn or Candy's tail.

Her back end sank under water and she started flailing her front legs and thrashing her head. She couldn't swim! I had never seen a horse that couldn't swim. I tightened my grip on the reins and tried to keep her head above water. One leg came down on my head and knocked me underwater. I kicked back up. A hoof hit my shoulder hard, another glanced my ear. I dodged another hit, still trying to hold her head up. Water was getting in her nose and she was snorting and rolling her body back and forth and trying to climb all over me. I went under again, this time with a mouthful of water. I came up gasping for air. The water roiled around us. Candy pawed harder, desperate to find solid ground. She was starting to push me around and under. I couldn't hold her up anymore. I could barely hold myself up. I let go of the reins.

By the time my boots hit soggy bottom, the muddy water had swallowed Candy. No burping bubbles marred its dark surface. I crawled up on dry land, my chest heaving with exhaustion. What felt like a twenty-minute struggle surely had been no more than five minutes. Hell, maybe three minutes. I was numb to the bruises I sustained, numb to the glory that had been in the day. Disaster had struck with the fury of a cyclone, a tidal wave, a horse that couldn't swim. How could a horse not swim? They were like dogs. Every dog can swim. Candy had tried to tell me she couldn't swim, but in my frustration and need to win the battle, I had failed to listen. I was not numb to the feel of being a fool and to having my heart broken by my own stubbornness.

I sloshed back the mile and half to headquarters in a flabbergasted fog. I could still see our trail through the grass. I had been out for a ride on a young, healthy, pretty horse and now she was dead. I stumbled my way over uneven ground, wet chaps swishing, boots sloshing, talking out loud trying to figure out the whole situation. If I had named her Squaw Piss would she have died? Probably. But I couldn't say for sure. All I knew was that I failed her. And here I was doing the cowboy walk of shame back to the ranch, my horse on the bottom of a stinking water hole. I was an idiot. I lost a horse and a friend. What kind of cowboy was I?

That day I was a jumble of recriminations—guilt, anger, regret. I was not in a place to learn. But in the following weeks and months, I looked hard at my role in Candy's death and acknowledged I had failed my horse by not paying attention. I vowed from that point on to be receptive to what my horses were telling me.

CHAPTER NINE

In Training

The day after the horses played ring-around-the-rosy with us in the horse pasture, I started the training. Monty Roberts and his horse-whispering manual had not yet appeared on the scene, and in my research and meanderings I never had bumped against anyone who trained a herd of wild horses. Training one adopted wild horse, maybe even two at a time, was business as usual. But training a group of a hundred, then another group and another, up to fifteen groups, up to fifteen hundred horses? Then merging them into one herd and getting that herd to follow men on horseback with no renegades blasting out? Even for a lifelong cowboy that was one heck of a wow. Yet I held to the belief that herd modification training would work with horses just as it had with cattle.

The four hundred head remained in the same corral where we penned them the day before. With another dose of difficulty, Russ, Marty, John, and I cut one hundred horses and drove them into the training arena. They gathered at the far end, a nervous bunch shaking their heads, shifting around as if threatened by shadows dancing on the ground. I gathered the cowboys at the opposite end. Anticipation filled our corner. I didn't want anyone to go out swinging like a hyped-up boxer, so I laid out a plan.

"Let's spread out and take it at a walk. No quick movements. Just ride toward the group." The three men, all professional horse handlers, nodded. "And at the same time, we're going to talk to them. Out loud. Real friendly." No one said a word. "You know," I said, "talk like you're sitting across from your buddy having a beer at the end of the day." Russ shifted slightly in his saddle and looked down. It's bad cowboy etiquette to roll your eyes at the boss. John looked thoughtful for a moment, then jogged his head as if the concept clicked. We were out to make friends, win the horses' trust. No yelling. No getting frustrated or angry. We headed out toward the jittery group.

"Easy does it. We're not going to hurt you."

"No need to get that wild look in your eyes."

"We're all friends here."

We had walked halfway down the corral, chatting steadily, when a bay mare at the edge of the bunch decided she'd had enough. She sprang into a run, headed for the opposite end of the arena, setting an example for the other ninety-nine mustangs. I pulled up on Clyde as horse after horse whizzed past, so close I could have reached out and touched them. The whites and darks of their eyes blurred into orbs of fright and suspicion. As abruptly as it started, the stampede stopped. The horses stood, for a moment more confused than afraid. Their run had been cut short by corral fencing. I turned the crew around.

"All right, here we come again. Let us get a few feet closer."

"Bay mare, why don't you stay in the bunch this time? It's a safe place to be."

"Steady, there. No need to bump each other."

"You horses, you're doin' great . . . uh oh, there you all go again."

It was a reenactment of Palomino Valley. Horses crowd in corner. Cowboys approach. Horses bolt to other corner. It would take time before these animals figured out our intentions. Fortunately the dimensions of the arena would give them no choice but to pay attention to us and listen to what we had to say. The memory of Roy's niggling voice tried to rebuke me for thinking wild horses could be trained. I muffled his words.

After twenty minutes of this back and forth, the mustangs started showing frustration and looked harassed. "Let's give 'em a break, guys," I said. We returned to the barn to unsaddle.

"Boy, they don't like to catch you looking at them," said John, dismounting. "More so than any horse I've ever trained."

"I'm not so sure those critters are ever going to be our friends," said Marty.

I settled my saddle on one of the cedar racks. "Well, we were able to get a few feet closer before they got ouchie." I poured some grain into Clyde's manger. I could see what lay at the heart of the training program—a massive amount of repetition and patience. We were about to become kindergarten teachers teaching a group of horses to follow the leader and not stray from the group. Teaching a horse like Aunt Jemima or Saber was high school level compared to this. Unlike cows, horses dribble out their trust. We needed to collect it with the patience of an Arizona rancher collecting rain in a gauge.

"I'll see you all back here in two hours," I said, rubbing on Clyde's neck. "We'll get in there and do it again." Russ looked perplexed. "It's all about the repetition, boys," I said. "Building trust through repetition. We'll keep getting in there every few hours until they wake up and realize we're not the enemy. That's the only way we're going to break them out of the races. Then, when they learn to follow us, we'll start taking them through gates and corrals, then into the lane, and finally push them into the pasture." I coated the words with confidence. "And remember this conversation because in four or five more days you'll see a whole different set of horses."

Of course, I had no idea how long it would take for the horses to change their behavior. One week? Ten days? Twenty days? We'd find out soon enough.

Two hours later, we returned to the barn, curried and saddled our horses. Over four hundred horse hooves again pounded the sand in the arena. Yet this time, we could get closer to them before they bolted. This was progress in my eyes, though nobody else commented on it. We again called it quits after twenty minutes.

At the start of round three, the horses were noticeably calmer. But my favorite bay mare bolted out of the group. I turned Clyde and charged after her. We ran her into a corner. "Get back in the bunch, you renegade bitch," I hollered, ten feet behind her. That shook her up. She wheeled around and hightailed it back into the bunch as fast as she had left it. Come spring, when we needed to move the entire herd six miles to fresh pasture, we didn't want any runaways. Lessons needed to be learned in the corral now, before the field trips started. Teaching feisty individuals that their comfort level was highest in a group and not on solo jaunts became an important part of the training.

"We can get one more session in before dark." I hung the bridle on a nail. "See you here in another two hours."

Before walking out of earshot, I heard Russ say, "Does he really think he's gonna train these broomtails?"

"Hell, he trained two thousand head of cattle. Nobody would believe that's possible," John said.

"Shit, man," said Russ. "This could take forever."

Marty replied, "As long as we can do it horseback."

I watched a broad-shouldered black-and-white paint flare his nostrils and puff out a soft snort. Some of the horses nearby cocked their ears back and echoed his recognition at seeing four familiar men on horseback enter the training arena. The mustangs' sentiment and behavior had shifted during the five days of training. They had graduated to following one of us in orderly fashion around the corral. The herd had begun to accept us as the alpha males. Even the bay mare that spooked and kept breaking away realized she couldn't go anywhere and no one was out to hurt her. The cowboys had accepted that this training would be their way of life for a while. No one griped. It was becoming as much a part of the job as feeding cattle every day. We just did it.

Clyde and I walked at an oblique angle toward the paint. "Hey there," I said, "did you get enough breakfast? There's plenty to go around this camp." I avoided direct eye contact. He flipped one ear forward and one ear back, then nodded his head and began a chewing motion with his lips even though his mouth was empty. What was he telling me? It almost looked like he had a grin on his face. "You keep talking to me and I'll figure out what you're saying. And I'll keep talking to you. It's not like we come from different planets. Right now, though, I'm thinking you're the smarter of us two."

Clyde and I walked past the happy guy and wove through a group of roans that insisted on hanging out together. If they got split up while running around the corral, they quickly found their way back together. Their coats, with the characteristic fine dusting of white, had started to turn darker, heralding the onset of winter. A few grunted at being interrupted from grazing on the hay. They took one or two steps to get out of my way. Being with the mustangs never jangled Clyde. He refused to let their glares and snorts antagonize him, and when they reared up or raced past, he stood his ground like a big brother inured to the antics of wilder siblings.

John threaded his way toward us. "Couldn't do this a couple of days ago, could we?" he said and grinned.

"They were wound way too tight," I said. A mare with the markings of a Pryor looked up from eating and turned to face us. She chewed her lips like the paint had done and pawed the ground with a front hoof. "Glad to see you're so interested," I said to her. Were she and the paint saying the same thing?

"I've noticed a couple other horses do that," John said. "Could this be their secret code of acceptance?"

By golly, of course. It made total sense. "You might have just

6. A wild mustang

hit the mother lode of this training system," I said, feeling a trill of excitement. "Cows acknowledged us by getting more gentle, but it's looking like these horses are giving us a high-five in their own language."

The horses seemed to be recognizing that we weren't like other men, who chased them with machines, trapped them in corrals, and did nothing to diminish their fear. Our training methods had opened the door to their world, and now they were saying hey, let's be friends. And on day four of the training. If only Red and Roy could see this.

It was time to move on to the next lesson: "Going through the Gate." Although the horses had passed through the gate to enter the training arena and had passed through numerous other gates, they remained timid about going through a new gate. I didn't know what invisible wire they saw or maybe felt when they ran through that open space. Since moving from pasture to pasture required going through gates, it was imperative they get over their fear. I gathered the crew.

"Russ, you start leading the horses around the corral. I'll open the gate and by the second pass, three of us will be ready to wing them through."

Russ rode around. The horses looked up. A rangy sorrel that often positioned herself in the front next to the bay mare started following him. The rest of the group fell into line. John, Marty, and I headed to the gate in the corner leading into another corral.

Russ and his horse trotted toward us towing the pack, and he went through the gate. The sorrel came up to it and stopped almost in midstride. It was like one of those cartoons where everyone starts bumping into each other. Within seconds it became a cluster of horses. Heads pushed up against rumps. There was a chorus of nervous neighs. The lead horses just stood and looked at the gate.

"Bring 'em around again," I yelled. John and Marty abandoned positions. Marty started out, got some of the horses to follow, and the pack loosened up.

"Guess they don't like the gate," said Russ, coming back through it.

I didn't have to think long about this melodrama. I knew exactly what to do. If you can't tell them, show them.

"Russ, as Marty comes around the corner, you jump in the lead with him and both of you go through the gate. Don't even pause. John and I will push on the back. Show these horses that's it's not a problem to go through. They'll see it's safe and they'll jump across." Russ looked at me like my brain cells had fallen into my boots. Ah well, he didn't have to believe me. I knew a horse could learn by watching.

When Russ swung in with Marty and went through the gate, John and I pushed hard on the back of the pack. The leaders paused for a second, then jumped over the barrier only they saw. The rest of the pack crowded through as fast as they could go, pushing and shoving, knocking the outside horses into the posts on either side. Eventually they were all through. I got off Clyde and shut

7. Horses pushing through a corral gate

the gate, happy to have crossed this barrier. I sent a silent thank you to Blondie, the horse that years back taught me her kind can learn by watching.

My partner in the Nebraska ranch, Allan Stratman, unexpectedly showed up one Saturday at Lazy B headquarters pulling a horse trailer behind his pickup. He had driven the three hours from Sonoita, Arizona, where he lived. I was in the house and saw him drive up and walked out to greet him. My eight-year-old daughter, Sarah, who had been playing nearby, and her dog Boots joined me.

"Hey, Al. How you doin'? Brought you and Sarah here a little something." Stratman opened the trailer door and backed out a quarter horse palomino mare. She was tall, about fifteen and a half hands, sleek, and beautifully put together with an intelligent head.

"Meet Blondie," he said, holding the lead rope out to Sarah. "She's about to move in with you."

Sarah looked at me as if I could explain away her puzzlement. I had no clue what was happening so answered with the same quizzical look. Sarah took the rope. "Hey, Blondie." Blondie lifted her head in quick acknowledgement, then turned to check out her surroundings.

Stratman explained that he bought Blondie six months ago. She came from a lineage of top-notch quarter horses. He had been trying to break her since. "But she's so hardheaded I've had next to no luck breaking her. Yesterday I got to thinking she just might be better off with a female trainer." He put a hand on Sarah's shoulder. "You're the finest young horsewoman I've ever seen and I think she belongs with you."

Sarah's eyes widened. "Do you want me to train her for you?"

"Nope. She's yours. I give her to you, and I wish you better luck than what I've had with her." Sarah looked as if she had been handed the biggest and best Christmas present from under the tree. Blondie looked down her muzzle at the small, pigtailed creature bouncing on the tips of her tennies.

With that and a brief visit, Santa Claus drove off over the horizon, a cloud of magical dust in his wake. We stood there awestruck, rubbing on our newest family member. Sarah already had the look of love.

"Go on," I said. "Get your boots. Let's see what this girl has to offer."

Stratman was right. Blondie could be a real butthead. Sarah wanted to train her to be a jumper because she loved horse jumping and the competition it offered. But that rebel of a mare had her own ideas about how the world works. She'd grab the bit in her teeth and cold jaw, then run off with Sarah, refusing to do what Sarah wanted. More than once, Blondie threw her head up and hit Sarah right in the face and hurt her. But Sarah never cried. In fact, Blondie couldn't do anything to make Sarah fear her or abandon the task of breaking her.

One day I came in from work and saw Sarah on Blondie. I went over to the corral to check on her.

"Dad, when I want her to gallop, she wants to buck. Here, watch." Sarah spurred her and Blondie jumped but not into a gallop. That horse went to bucking across the corral. I couldn't do a thing but watch and be ready to scoop up Sarah if she flew off. Halfway across the corral, Sarah looked back at me, grinning. "Look, Dad, isn't she cute?" It was one female will against another and Sarah was determined to win.

Another day, I noticed the two of them in the jumping arena.

"How's it going, Sar?"

"Dad, I can get Blondie to jump the regular jumps with the poles across, but not the roll top." They must have been working at it for a while because she sounded frustrated. The roll top was solid and wide but only three feet high, the same height as the pole jumps Blondie easily cleared. "Can you help me?"

"Run her at it and show me what she does."

Sarah rode straight at the jump. Blondie stopped right in front of it. The next time, Blondie veered right. Every time Sarah tried to jump her over the roll top, Blondie refused.

I had an idea. I hauled over two corral panels from the shed and set one at either end of the roll top at an angle, creating a V to prevent Blondie from veering. It didn't take that horse but a few runs to figure out that she could turn in front of the panels. If Sarah managed to get her inside the wings, Blondie stopped at the roll top and refused to jump. Sarah tried this and that, all to no avail. The frustration factor was beginning to multiply. Without saying anything to Sarah, I picked up a piece of old plastic pipe lying on the ground and got in position near the jump. Sarah lined up Blondie and started riding her. The second Blondie started to stop, I swatted her a good one right across the hips. Blondie jumped about twenty feet forward, but not over the roll top. Sarah landed behind the saddle but didn't fall off.

"Dad! What are you doing? Don't hurt my horse."

"I'm not hurting her," I said. "I wanted to see if I could change her mind. This is a test of wills. Your will says one thing, and hers says another."

"But that's not the way to do it," said Sarah. She scrambled back in the saddle, adding some further tongue lashes.

We worked with Blondie for a while longer without success. By this time, all of us had lost our temper. Blondie had her head set in every direction but over the jump. Sarah was angry with Blondie but angrier with me, and I was angry with Blondie for being so stubborn. We were locked up in a box of frustration with no productive place to go. I pushed my mind out of the box, breathed in some fresh air, and did some thinking. Sarah tried the jump again. Blondie stopped short again.

"Is Squaw in the corral?" I asked. Squaw was Sarah's other horse.

"Yes," said Sarah.

"Go get her. I'll stand here and hold Blondie. When you get back, I want you to take the roll top with Squaw. I'm going to have Blondie watch you jump."

Sarah stuck out her chin. "That's a dumb idea. Blondie's not going to jump just by watching another horse do it."

"Sarah, do you have a better idea? We're all angry and we're up against the wall here. I don't have another idea, but if you have one, now's the time to lay it out. Otherwise go get Squaw and let's try it. I agree it probably won't work, but maybe it will give us time to cool off." Sarah rolled her eyes, but she dismounted and huffed off to get Squaw.

She returned to the arena leading Squaw with Boots in tow. Wherever Sarah and Squaw went, Boots went, so Sarah, Squaw, and Boots all took the roll top.

"Now turn around and jump it coming the other way."

"This is stupid," Sarah muttered. Yeah, it probably is, but I didn't admit it out loud.

8. Sarah and Blondie

The threesome prepared to jump. I squeezed Blondie's halter and forced her head in Sarah's direction. "Now you pay attention to this, you hardheaded bitch. Look how Squaw jumps that." No response from Blondie.

"Do it again," I said.

Sarah, Squaw, and Boots jumped four more times each way. I kept a tight grip on Blondie and told her each time to pay attention. She quietly stood her ground.

"Let's try Blondie now." Sarah rode Squaw over and swapped lead ropes with me. "Boots, stay here," I said.

The three of us watched as Sarah and Blondie readied and started toward the jump. When Blondie came to the roll top, she shifted her weight onto her back legs and pushed off the ground. She cleared that jump like she had done it a hundred times before. Sarah quickly turned her and jumped her the other direction, just to make sure it wasn't a fluke. She jumped her again and again. Boots and I joined Sarah and Blondie for a little congratulatory hoopla.

The switch had flipped in Blondie, and with the flip came the pledge of allegiance. From that day forward, Blondie acquiesced to Sarah's every bidding—not just with jumping. Blondie was eager to read Sarah's mind and did just that as often as possible. She and Sarah went on to win so many shows I lost count.

CHAPTER TEN

Renegades

The Suburban bounced over the ground in the meadow east of headquarters. The snow had melted and the soil underneath the tires had a new give to it. The sky had decided to wear its blues instead of grays, but a wicked spring wind had kicked up after breakfast, so I opted to check on the horses from inside a heated truck. It wasn't as if I hadn't been getting fresh air. I had spent almost the entire winter at the sanctuary, and except for Sundays and a few days lost to a snowstorm, the cowboys and I had been on horseback every day in the training arena. When conditions became slick, we took the pace down a notch.

Driving through the herd, I felt optimism surge. The sun highlighted the horses, now twelve hundred strong, creating a canvas of golds, bronzes, beiges, blacks, and deep browns that stretched out before me. This entire gang had graduated from training school. Every one of these mustangs had learned to follow a lead horse through corral gates, then into the wide lanes separating corrals from pastures, and finally into the horse pasture or meadow. Best of all, we had become friends, bonded in part by mutual trust. If we left them for a week, then came to gather them, we had a controlled game of follow-the-leader rather than a day at the races. On May tenth we would take the horses from headquarters to summer grazing. It was a six-mile journey to Mud Lake and we needed the horses to stay in a group. I suspected the herd could handle the journey now, but I didn't mind having another six weeks to reinforce the training.

I drove slowly, keeping an eye out for injuries, limps, or a pregnant mare having trouble delivering. I passed a mama, a light-gray mare, and her dark-haired baby, one of the first foals to drop. This time of year was special. We weren't sure how many babies to expect. As it turned out, sixty would be born by early May. Ahead the big black-and-white paint had assumed his usual position near the edge of the herd. He was handsome and regal and always caught the attention of anyone viewing the horses. John had taken to calling him Happy.

I squinted into the sun. Were horses on the wrong side of the fence? Four stood looking right at me. Well son-of-a-gun. Those suckers were in Randy Campbell's pasture. Now how in the world had they gotten there?

I turned the Suburban toward the fence. Happy looked up as I drove by and chewed a greeting. While going through training about two-thirds of the herd acknowledged us in this way and continued to do so, though not every time we interacted with them. I rolled down the window. "Wouldn't want to give me the scoop on those renegades, would you?" He tilted his ears forward as the wind swooped up my words. On the opposite side of the fence, one of the four, a big dun, shook her head up and down as if laughing, then took off at a run up the nearest hill. Up and over she went, accomplices close behind. Oh great, they were playing hooky.

I steered the truck along the fence line. No broken wires or fallen posts. No open gates. Those horses must have jumped out. What needled me more than having to be the truant officer and go out and collect them was the fact that they were trained. They knew better than to leave the herd. What was going on here? Were these horses part of the one-third that never spoke to us using the mustang code of friendship? Would the rest of this group revert to their wild ways and start jumping fences? I shivered, rolled up the window, and cranked the heat to melt the heavy thought out of my mind.

Back at headquarters, I found John and Alan Jr. leaning over the engine of a tractor. Alan Jr. had come up from Arizona for the week, something he liked to do every month or so, and had been amazed at the horses' progress. Until twenty minutes ago, I had shared his awe. I related what happened.

John stood up and wiped his hands on a rag. "Well, darn. Didn't want to hear that news," he said. "I thought they were all good and trained." He tossed the rag to Alan Jr. and slammed down the tractor hood. "I'll go saddle up after lunch and see if I can't bring those badasses back."

The shadows were already lengthening by the time John came riding across the meadow, shoulders drooped. "He didn't get those horses gathered," I said to Al. I had a cold beer waiting for him in the doublewide. John leaned against the kitchen counter and took a healthy swig.

"Those four head, man, they are one stubborn group. They sure did default back to their skittish state." He sounded like a father disappointed in his children's behavior. "One rider can't take them. I blew through that meadow back and forth more times than I care to count and never got them to turn. We're going to need a crew to outflank them." He suggested that Russ, Alan Jr., and I slip around the group on the east side, while he would cross the creek pasture and flank them on the other side. "We'll leave the meadow gate open and when they run from us, they'll run right back into the herd." He shot his empty hand forward like it was taking off down a runway.

I took a sip of scotch and considered the idea. The wild turkeys marched past the window headed for their nighttime roost. Whatever was going to happen it would have to happen tomorrow.

"What do you think, Al?" I asked my son. Though fairly quiet, he had a way of coming up with the right answer at the right time.

"Well, Dad, we have those good motorcycles here. I'd love to blow the rust out of their pipes a little. Why don't I take one of the fast ones and show those rascals how to run? Maybe I can bend them and get them back into the herd."

We had used the motorcycles—wide-tired dirt bikes—while training each group of horses. We would walk the bikes into the arena, fire them up, and wind through the herd. Motorcycles come in handy on a ranch, so I wanted the animals to get accustomed to the sound and sight of them. Although they didn't like the snarly beasts, they grudgingly accepted them. I didn't want to rely on the bikes; I wanted to keep things as natural as possible. Since most of the mustangs had been freaked out by loud motors at some point in their past, I tried to avoid having them relive that horror. But now four recalcitrant animals were throwing a challenge directly in our faces.

I weighed Alan Jr.'s plan against John's. The trainer in me needed to teach those horses a lesson, to show them that their safest place was in the middle of the herd. The speed of a dirt bike might just help ingrain that concept. Alan had raced cycles extensively in high school and was clearly the best rider among us. A part of me acknowledged my hypocrisy for preaching against helicopters, then using motorcycles for the same purpose. At least a dirt bike didn't have near the noise of a chopper. Besides, we might learn something new.

"Go for it," I said to my son.

The next morning Alan groomed the cycle, topped off the tank, oiled the chain, donned helmet and gloves, and set out on his mission.

I stayed busy at my desk and kept one eye on the clock. A little before noon, I walked outside thinking it time to get in the Suburban and go look for him, but there he was, putting back up the meadow. I met him on the side of the shed where we stored the bikes. His jeans were muddy almost up to the knee. Maybe the ground was softer than I had thought. He told his story over lunch in John's kitchen.

Even before he opened the gate to Randy's pasture, Al saw the horses. When he drove through, they took off in a high run to the east. He set out in hot pursuit. The horses ran, ducking and dodging through the hills and vales. Al would pull up alongside and try to turn them, but they refused to be turned. He tried a few more times but realized his efforts would continue to be futile. These were smart, stubborn SOBs. So he tried something a little different. While driving parallel to them, he pushed just a bit. They, in response, turned just a bit. He kept at it, patiently pushing, little by little getting them to bend how he wanted them. He became so engrossed in the task that when the horses ran on one side of a small rise, he stayed on course with them and zipped over the center of the hill. Suddenly he found himself airborne and looming above a large pond. He splashed smack-dab in the middle of the waist-high muddy water. The motorcycle sank out of sight. I could just see the horses snickering as they ran off. Al managed to push the cycle through the spongy mud onto shore.

We always carried tools under the seat, so he pulled out the spark plug, then dried it and the wires going to it. An hour later, the cycle fired up and he was off again. He probably was freezing, but he also was determined. He found those four head. This time they responded to him and turned. He said they seemed glad to go through the gate and ran pell-mell into the main herd. Maybe they were happy to get away from the wild, noisy demon. Maybe they finally recognized the calming safety of the herd. Maybe they were tired of running. Regardless, they learned something because they never ran away or jumped a fence again.

Two horses must have been understudies for those four head. A chestnut and a palomino soon followed and jumped over the fence. Not just once or twice, but every day. There they would be on the other side of the fence, taunting us. We'd have to spend time getting them back through the gate. After three weeks of these antics, my patience wore thin. "Let's bring the herd through the lanes and cut those two out," I told John. It was time for some remedial training.

It took us a couple of hours to gather the herd and push them through the lanes. As the two naughty renegades went through, we switched the gates and pushed them into the corrals. John and Marty managed to get each in a separate small corral.

I rode into the first corral feeling like a boxer going into a cage fight. The corral was so small that when we entered, the mustang freaked. She started running around bug-eyed and crazy, rearing up and racing side to side. Clyde and I stood our ground at one end, moving as little as possible. My senses were on high alert. I kept Clyde facing the mare and watched for the start of an attack. I watched her ears, the tension in her muscles, her body language. Never did I allow my fear or nervousness to surface. Either of those would have been a magnet for an attack. The entire time I talked. Gentle, firm, encouraging words. After thirty or forty minutes, the horse, now foamy with sweat, started to calm down. Her sides heaved and she sent out a string of snorts, but she listened to me. Clyde and I could approach a few steps without her having a tantrum. At the end of the hour- and-a-half session she was exhausted. As was I. I turned her back out into the herd and repeated the same routine with the other horse.

The two horses never reached the point in the corral where they would bob their heads in acknowledgement, one ear forward and one ear up, or chew their mouths or paw their front legs. Their pride got in the way. They were more like reformed teenagers, too stubborn to admit their erroneous ways but no longer eager to disrupt the class. Later I could spot them in the herd. They were content to hang in the middle, not at the edge. My will won those battles and the outcome was positive for all. That hadn't always been the case in my life. My proof was Tequila and the day that started with a simple phone call.

"When are you gonna come get your bull? He's tramplin' our cotton plants and almost lives in our alfalfa." Charlie Clouse didn't sound angry, just a little frustrated.

"I'd be happy to, but what are you talking about, Charlie?" I said into the phone. Charlie owned a farm down on the Gila River across from Lazy B.

"One of your bulls has been jumping the fence," he said.

This was news to me. Apparently, for the past year, this bull would hightail it over the fence and maraud through the fields, crushing cotton plants, feasting on alfalfa, and making a general mess of things. Charlie would run him into the thickets by the river, where he would hide until Charlie disappeared. Then the naughty guy would jump the fence again and the cycle would repeat.

"Why didn't you tell me about this sooner? I would have come and gotten him." I felt a prickle of irritation. I could already tell this bull had taught himself well. He had the upper hand and was working the system. Now we'd have to retrain him, if that was even possible. Charlie wanted to know how we were going to get him. "Will you rope him if you have to? Because that's one big sucker of a bull."

"Yeah, Charlie, if I need to rope him, I will." I didn't particularly want to rope a full-grown bull, but if that was the only way to gather him, I would do it. Shooting him wasn't an option.

"Then tell me when you're gonna do it cuz I'll stay home from work. I want to see this one."

Oh good grief. What were we running, a rodeo? "Stay home tomorrow, Charlie, and we'll come get that bull."

If Saber had been in my string, I would have chosen him for the job but this was the pre-Saber era, so the next morning I went out and caught Tequila, a young mare with mousy, grulla coloring

9. Tequila

that I was riding at the time. She was Candy's older sister but from the start was a sweet, kind gal. She had a big, solid frame, with strong shoulders, and never shied away from work. She liked to work cattle but wasn't a top-notch cow horse or particularly athletic. We had never been in a situation together that demanded she give everything; thus I didn't know her limits. Since she was the biggest horse in my string, I chose her for the job hoping she could handle it. I recruited Cole Webb, our foreman, and Vince Sanchez, a Lazy B cowboy, to accompany me. Cole's horse was smaller than Tequila, but I didn't think that would pose a problem. Vince would work the corral gate on foot. We saddled the horses, loaded them in the trailer, drove over to the Clouse farm, and parked near an old corral adjacent to the cotton field. The plan was to run the bull in there, then load him in the trailer.

The corral was cluttered with wood and debris and had loose rub boards hanging down. I assigned Vince cleanup duty. Cole and I headed our horses out along the levy that separated the Gila

River from Charlie's fields. A barbed wire fence ran the length of the levy. The ground on both sides of the fence was a mosaic of giant hoofprints. We opened a gate to get to the river where we thought the bull might be hanging out and left it open so we could backtrack through it. The ground had long since gulped the monsoon rains so the slender river barely filled one-eighth of its quarter-mile bed. Thickets of scrub brush and mesquite grew in the sand, perfect hideouts for a crafty animal not quite crafty enough to hide his trail. We followed a fresh track of prints that led straight into a thicket.

There was a muted drum roll of thudding hooves, a splash of water, and a big red bull with a massive set of horns jumped out front and center about eighty yards ahead of us. Except for the tips having been cut off the horns years before, he could have been the poster bull for Merrill Lynch. He must have weighed eighteen hundred pounds. He glared at us, defiant, then bolted into the next thicket. He might have been all hulk, but he was quicker than an NFL running back.

Cole and I loped toward him, hoping to haze him out of the thicket. Instead he raced downstream to the next clump of brush. We approached and he dashed out, ran across the river, and ducked behind more mesquite and sagebrush. This tacking back and forth across the river with him getting the better of us quickly grew tiresome. I decided to call a different play. I hand signaled to Cole that I was going to slip around to the far side of brush where the bull would exit. Cole knew the play. He stayed on the opposite side and started making a racket. The bull burst out. He looked startled to see me twenty yards away. The lid popped off the action box.

Tequila charged the bull. I threw my rope, intending to rope him around the neck so I could choke him if I had to. A bull can't fight if he can't breathe. But instead, the rope pulled up around his horns. I dallied up. Tequila jammed her front legs straight out. The bull turned and headed off, dragging her twelve hundred pounds like a sled in a southwestern Iditarod. A hundred yards later he stopped to catch his breath. Cole rode up on the side of him and hazed him toward the corral. For the next twenty minutes, the fight spread over the river valley. When the bull turned toward the corral, we gave him slack and followed him. Then he'd tire, stop, and turn back toward us. Not what you want. A feisty bull facing you. Cole would fight him again until he turned forward again and we'd make more progress. I could feel Tequila beginning to tire. I was sorry that I had roped this sucker; it was more than Tequila could handle, but she wasn't going to quit. She remained brave and stayed with the job.

"Come on, girl. I can see the corral." The bull jerked the rope and I let him pull us. "Cole, you take the rope," I yelled. It seemed like a good point to give Tequila a break. I loosened the taut rope and threw Cole the slack; he dallied on his saddle horn. The bull must have felt the rope's tension change, because as soon as Cole dallied up that big old lug took off, practically pulling Cole's horse on her nose. Her nine hundred pounds were no match for his brute strength. I could see this was a mistake.

The bull climbed up the levee and veered through the open gate. Tequila and I galloped up next to Cole and reclaimed the rope. Tequila gave it another all. She grunted, tightened her shoulders, leaned back, and locked her legs. The bull slowed, but didn't stop. He was furious that he was still roped and in a fix. He hunched forward and stomped down the levee toward the cotton field. Out of the corner of my eye, I noticed a red dirt bike at the edge of the field. I could see two teenagers in a row of cotton, hoeing weeds. They must have arrived while we were chasing the bull in the riverbed.

The bull caught site of the cycle and made a beeline for it. Tequila lost her leverage and galloped behind him. That ornery beast made for the bike as if he was a bull in a Spanish ring charging the matador's red cape. One of the boys stood up and pointed. "Hey, that's our bike," he hollered. "Leave it alone." They started running toward it.

"Get away. I can't control him," I yelled, motioning them to turn back. I could feel the bull's strength and determination pulling the rope. All I could do was hang on and pray he was more interested in the bike than the boys.

The bull never paused. He ran right up to that motorcycle, hooked his horns under it, and tossed it in the air like it was a play toy. Everything halted—the boys, the bull, Tequila, Cole—except the bike. We watched that two-wheeler fly twenty feet in the air, then plummet toward earth. It landed with a metal-crunching thud. The boys took off running in the opposite direction. Shit. They probably saved up a year's salary of cotton-hoeing money to buy that motorcycle. Now there it lay, crumpled to death.

The bull shook his head, snorted, and stamped a few times. Tequila raised her head. She wasn't going to let him get the last laugh if she could help it. He looked around as if contemplating what more damage he could do. He charged forward, jerking Tequila. She followed for a few steps, then splayed her feet and leaned back as hard as she could. I could feel her shoulders shake.

"Hang in there, girl," I said. "Maybe he'll head for the corral."

Her quivering muscles told me her shoulders were sore and she was having a hard time holding the bull. She couldn't dig in enough and we had to give slack when he pulled. Desperation hovered around the scene. If I let the bull go, he could turn and charge Cole or me or run after the boys. None of us wanted to see an angry, horned, one-ton animal barreling toward him. I heard a motor sputtering behind me. I turned in the saddle enough to see Charlie Clouse coming up the levee on his old popping Johnny, a 4020 John Deere tractor with a front-end loader. He must have seen our predicament because he wheeled in through the gate and pulled up beside me.

"Looks like the battle's in full swing," he shouted. "Can I help out?"

"Lord, I hope so. We're just about overmatched here." The bull stopped and turned to look at us, deciding whether to go forward or retrace his steps toward us. Charlie accelerated. He steered the tractor in front of Tequila and bumped that old bull none too gently. The bull wheeled around and took off straight toward the corral. Our convoy followed at high speed. Along the edge of the cotton field we went, then the alfalfa field. The bull stopped abruptly and looked back. Charlie was on him with the John Deere, and off the bull ran, not happy about being bumped again. The alfalfa field bordered the corral.

"Tequila, we gotta get him in the corral." She pulled back a little, tightening the rope. The bull pulled to the right in response. If he kept on running, he'd go through the corral gate in less than a minute.

Vince stood at the ready, both hands on the open gate. Cole hazed the bull on one side and Charlie rode the tractor close on the other side. That big old red bull was running straight as an arrow. I unwound the dally and held the rope in my hand. The bull ran through the corral gate. I tossed the rope in behind him and Vince slammed the gate shut.

The bull stopped in the middle of the small corral. He swung his head in both directions, stomped around in a one-eighty, and went to snorting and pawing. He was one pissed-off dude at having lost the battle.

"Tequila, you get the purple heart," I said, patting her shoulder. I was so proud of the way she hung in there to the very end. If I had known it was going to be such a huge chore, I wouldn't have subjected her to it. Every once in a while I bit off more than I could chew and this was one of those times. I dismounted and let the reins drop. She wasn't going anywhere. She was exhausted, sore, and used up. My heart went out to her. "You'll get extra grain tonight, sweetheart, after we get this bad boy home." I rubbed on her neck and nose.

Charlie, Cole, Vince, and I spent the next quarter hour trying to get the bull up the loading chute into the trailer. We swung long sticks in front of him, yelled, did everything we could think of. If we had had a red cape, we would have stood at the top of the chute and waved it. But that gol-darn animal stood his ground, flames jumping out of his eyes, looking for something to vent his fury on. When the mercury on our frustration thermometer began to top out, Vince volunteered to do the insane.

"I'll run across the corral," he said, like he had done it before a dozen times. "He's going to charge me. But just before I get to the chute, I'll jump for the fence. The bull will run under me and up the chute. Problem solved." He shrugged his shoulders like it was no big deal.

Vince was fast and young, but this was Mr. Macho he was talking about, stud of the bull kingdom. I said, "You sure you want to do that? I've seen this guy run and you can be damn sure he'll give you a chase."

Vince eyed his competitor. He gave another casual cowboy shrug that said risking his life was no big deal. "I can do it, Boss. How else are we going to get him up that ramp?"

Standing there in the heat of a stalemate, I couldn't answer his question. "Okay," I said, my glass of confidence half-empty. "But put some fire in those boots."

Vince slipped around to the other side of the corral and climbed over the fence. He hit the ground running and yelling. He ran like a jackrabbit, but that bull's muscles were spring-loaded and ready to snap. He lurched into a run. Vince threw a hand and foot on the fence at the same time the bull hiked his horns under Vince's butt. Vince became airborne and went flying over the corral fence, head over tail. I winced. He thumped down on his back. The bull surveyed his work and clopped up the wooden chute into the trailer.

Vince didn't move for a few moments. The wind in him had to be knocked from here to Lazy B. Cole hustled to secure the bull in the trailer, and Charlie and I jogged over to Vince prepared to give first aid. Before we got to him, Vince stood up, wobbled a step, and said with a grin, "Got that sonofabitch, didn't I?"

"You practicing to be a rodeo clown?" said Charlie, slapping him on the back.

I was glad he was in one piece.

Back at Lazy B, we unloaded the bull into his own corral where he stomped around for the rest of the day.

I led Tequila out of the trailer. She limped her way into the horse corral. "You stay here for a rest, girl. Eat some hay, take it easy." I put a hand on each shoulder and rubbed. I didn't like to see her in pain. "I couldn't be more proud of you, Tequila. You gave me everything you had and never quit even when it got down and dirty." She nosed my shirt.

We left the bull in the corral. Every time I looked his way, he got pissed and made me understand that he was not the forgiving type. He had lost his way of life and wasn't going to give in to rehab easily. Every few days, one of the cowboys would load hay in the pickup, drive it into the corral, and get out to throw it in the feed manger. That bull would charge and he'd have to jump back in the truck. I made a judgment call to never turn that animal out again. If we did and went to gather him, he might charge us or catch someone unaware and really do some damage. The following week I loaded him into the trailer and hauled him to the livestock auction. He made a lot of hamburger for someone.

Charlie told me who the kids were that owned the motorcycle. I called them and said if you can't fix your motorcycle, I'll buy you a new one. And that's what I ended up doing.

I gave Tequila a week in the corral and fed her extra hay. She walked around with a stiff gait, a sign of strained shoulder muscles. I thought it best to give her a long rest, so I turned her out for six months in the horse pasture, then brought her in, but she was still lame. Her shoulders had not healed right and she walked with a limp. I felt twinges of sadness and regret every time I looked at her. She was still handsome and young, much too good a horse to sell, so I turned her out with the broodmares to raise colts, and she raised some really fine ones.

CHAPTER ELEVEN

A Wormy Mess

John caught up with me in the shop where I was repairing a windmill part. "Found another dead horse this morning," he said. "On the northeast end of the meadow. It must have died last night because it wasn't out there yesterday when we passed through. Coyotes already had it skinned to the bones."

This wasn't news I wanted to hear. Last week two horses died, and two others the week before. Counting the one today that brought the total to five head dead in two weeks. That was more than coincidence or the result of old age. Something was amok in windswept paradise. I pushed the windmill blade into position on the band and pinched my finger. "Goddamnit," I said, both to the pinch and the mystery of the horses dying. "We've got to get to the bottom of this."

John suggested I call Doc Burford, cousin to Bob Burford, head of the BLM. He was reputed to be the best horse vet in the area. Over the phone we devised a plan. Anyone who found a dead horse on the ranch was to radio headquarters and stay with the carcass to keep the coyotes at bay. Whoever was at headquarters would call Doc Burford, who agreed to drop what he was doing and hightail it out to conduct a postmortem on the horse. It didn't take but two days before I put in the call to the vet's office.

Doc Burford arrived within two hours. We hopped in his truck and bounced out to the meadow. He cast an experienced eye over the herd as we drove through it.

"Well, these horses look fine. Beautiful, in fact," he added. They did look fine with their coats shining in the sun, calmly grazing on the blanket of newly sprouted grass. A bubble of pride floated up in me.

Near the northeast corner, I could see Russ waving us down. Doc pulled the truck up alongside a palomino mare. She lay on her side, legs out, head back. She wasn't thin and didn't look unhealthy in any way. She just looked like she was sleeping.

The back of Doc's truck was a hospital on wheels. He opened compartments and laid out his instruments on the hinged door that flipped out, then put on a rubber bib and pulled on latex gloves up to his elbows. He asked us to roll the horse on her back and spraddle the front and back legs. Choosing a butcher's skinning knife and starting at the brisket, he made a neat cut all the way down through the stomach clear to her bag. He skinned the hide back a good twelve inches on each side. Another cut opened up the gut cavity. He started pulling out entrails, stomach first, followed by small intestine.

"Hold your nose," he said, as he sliced through the stomach. The stench of partially digested food hit the air. With a gloved hand, he pulled out a handful of greenish matter. "Uh oh," he said. "See these?" He flicked a tiny translucent speck among the pieces of wet hay and grass. "These are worms. Not the kind that kill, but often the kind that accompany the killers. Let's check out the small intestine and find out what's hiding there."

He sliced the intestine, reached in, pulled out fecal matter, and examined it. "Just as I suspected. Here's what's killing your horses." I could see worms moving. "You have several types of worms, but this one here," he said, pointing, "this is the one that kills."

"Have the worms developed since she arrived, which might have been five months ago?" I asked.

"No, it takes worms a long time to multiply, so this horse definitely was infected well before you received her."

My background didn't give me much knowledge about worm infection. At Lazy B we never needed to worm because the dry climate was a natural deterrent. Worms can't survive in dust. Was it possible that worms were threatening the lives of twelve hundred horses?

"So what do we do now?"

Doc Buford snapped off his gloves. "You need to worm the horses. All of them, because you don't know which ones are infected and which ones aren't. And you need to do it right away. There are several different methods of worming. If it were only one horse, you could put a tube down its throat and inject the serum into the stomach. But with this large a herd, you don't want to head catch each one. I recommend Ivomec. It's a full-spectrum wormer and you can inject it into the muscle of the shoulder or neck. It's a bit more expensive, but every bit as effective."

John and I looked at each other, neither of us able to speak. In less than ten minutes, Doc Buford nailed the problem and it was a biggie. The thermostat of frustration had just been turned up. The BLM had sent me wormy horses. My contract with them called for them to deworm the horses before shipping. Where in the bureaucratic maze did that one get lost? Not only did this breach of contract affect the horses, it affected the land, which in turn threatened my code of honor to always leave the land better than I had found it. I wasn't a worm expert, but any rancher knows the cycle of worms. They grow in the horses, drop to the ground in the horses' poop, bury themselves in the soil, hatch as flies, sting the horses, and implant their larvae under the horses' skin. But as a result of someone's carelessness, the unwanted insects had taken up residence on Mustang Meadows Ranch and now horses were dying on my watch.

First thing I did after thanking Doc Burford was order the Ivomec.

It would arrive by Monday. John assured me we had a sufficient supply of vaccine guns. Next I called the BLM office in Sturgis.

"I've got a disaster here," I said to the voice at the other end. "You sent me wormy horses. I'm going to have to worm the entire herd, because someone in the shipping department didn't worm all of them and there's no way of tracking which ones have been wormed and which haven't."

After hearing my story, the voice proceeded to say that oh no, the horses can't be wormed now. There's no money.

"Well, I'm worming them next Tuesday."

The voice: "We can't get the Ivomec there that soon, and besides, you can't worm all those horses in one day. There are too many. It'll take you five days."

"No," I said, "that's not the plan. We're going to worm them on Tuesday. I've already ordered the Ivomec and it will be here by then. Furthermore, it won't take us a full day. I've trained the horses. We'll line them up in the chute and we'll just reach over and vaccinate them as they go by. We'll be done by two o'clock."

The voice rose. "Look, we've been in the horse business for forty years. Wild horses don't go up the chute that easily. Every time one gets turned around, you have to unload the whole chute and start fresh. You might even need a week."

"No," I said, "I've trained these horses. I know they'll file through without doing that." The voice wanted to argue.

"Look," I said, interrupting the cycle of this conversation. "I already ordered the vaccine and I intend for you to pay for it because this mess is your mistake. We're scheduled to vaccinate next Tuesday. If you want your people to learn something, send some representatives down. They can get up on the fence and watch, but they have to stay out of our way."

I slammed down the phone. The breeze blew in one window and out the other. I'm sure my words were scattered all over headquarters.

Tuesday arrived along with three BLM reps. I was setting up the vaccinating station in the back of the Suburban, parked alongside the chute. I went over and greeted the men and offered coffee but had no takers. I pointed out an unobtrusive place where they could stand and have a clear view of the action.

Everyone had his assignment. Russ would load the vaccine guns, ten doses per gun. John was horseback and would feed the horses into the rear of the chute. Carlos and Ramon would work the gates. Marty and I would vaccinate.

A dozen horses filed into the chute and Carlos shut the gate behind them. I pushed the needle into the first horse's shoulder and squeezed the handle of the vaccinating gun. Click. Done. Just like giving someone a punch on the shoulder. I walked toward the next horse in the chute. The horse flinched slightly as I inserted the needle. Squeeze. Click. Next horse. Squeeze, click. After ten horses and one minute, my gun was empty. Marty took over with his gun and I walked over to Russ to pick up a freshly loaded gun. When Marty was done, I took over. And so it went for five hours. We didn't use alcohol and rub. We did it cowboy style. There was no small talk. We started at nine and at quarter to two, I handed the guns to John, and he went straight to the bunkhouse to disassemble them and sanitize all the parts. I walked over to talk to the BLM reps, who hadn't budged.

"You put on a heck of a show," one of them said.

His coworker chimed in. "We expected to see horses balk and run. But golly, they marched through it like they had done this ten times before."

"Well we've worked with them quite a little," I said. If only they knew. "We've made friends and when we ask them to do something, they pretty much oblige."

"Boy, these corrals lend themselves to letting the horses flow through them. Could you train us to handle horses like that?"

Yes, I could, but I didn't tell them that. I was pleased at the day's results but still pissed so I let loose a cocky answer. "Strange that you've been in the wild horse business for forty years and I've been in it for six months and you're asking me if I can teach you? What's wrong with this picture?" It was a stupid thing to say.

"Well, we'll tell the boss how well this went today. He might want to have you give some classes on horse handling."

No one from the BLM ever called. Maybe if I courted them a little they would have. Maybe not. As it was, we had to vaccinate each year after that. We never had a problem with worms again, nor with the BLM putting up a stink about paying. They paid for all the vaccines, including the Ivomec we used that day. I don't know what level they had to climb up to in order to find the money, but they did. Or maybe they didn't have to climb at all. What mattered most was that we intercepted a disaster.

No cowboy likes to have a sick—or worse, dead—horse. But the reality is that it's as impossible for all ranch horses to stay healthy as it is for all human beings. Sickness and health are part of nature. What makes a difference is how you deal with each.

We didn't breed too many black horses at Lazy B, but we had a few and, by far, my favorite was Blackberry. Often black horses have white stockings or a star on their forehead. Not Blackberry. She was pure black and shiny. What really set her apart, however, was her demeanor. When we weaned her, she was the quickest of the group to respond to petting and gentleness. If she noticed me walk into the corral, she sauntered over to say hello and rested her head on my shoulder while I rubbed on her neck. If I was working on the other side of the fence, she came over to see what was up, a curious, intelligent look in her eyes. Always eager to please, she quickly learned to lead and load in a trailer. Once she and the other colts learned these basics, they moved up to Robb's Well.

All the Lazy B horses spent at least a year at Robb's Well, a hilly place with grass poking through a ground cover of rocks and boulders. We turned them out there and let them fend for themselves on what nature provided. Sure, we could have kept them at the corrals, ridden, fed, and cared for them, and they would have grown even larger, but we bred some pretty big horses as it was. There was a factor that overrode size and availability. The cogs of a busy, fully operating, 198,000-acre ranch are greased by self-reliance. Our horses needed to know how to traverse rocky terrain because they most likely would be doing that for the rest of their lives. They needed to learn to endure the heat of high-desert summers and adjust to the short but deep chill of winter, all beneath a giant roof of clear sky. They needed to learn to subsist on native ranch grass, not on the grain and hay that pampered horses receive when kept in stalls and corrals. Was it tough love? For sure. Were our horses loved? Just as kids with eight or nine siblings are loved by parents, grandparents, and a hoard of aunts and uncles, these rock-raised horses were loved too. In all my years of ranching, we didn't lose even a one of those horses out at Robb's Well to disease or predators.

One day Cole Webb and I went out to repair a well and decided to drive by the pasture to check on the colts and fillies, something we periodically did. The horses were scattered around the hillside, grazing. All appeared copacetic until I focused the binoculars on Blackberry. She had developed a limp. Cole and I got out of the truck to investigate. Blackberry noticed us and started to half-walk, half-trot unevenly down the hill toward us.

"Hey girl," I said, rubbing her nose. "What's going on with you?" She did a full-body shake as if trying to shake off the problem, whatever it was.

"It's her right shoulder," said Cole. I stepped around to look. Sure enough, at the bottom of her shoulder was a weeping wound about an inch wide. The hair around it had crusted over. "Looks like a puncture wound," he said. Besides being the ranch foreman,

PART 2

Cole served as our self-trained ranch doctor. "We're going to need to bring her in and see what's stuck in there."

We went back and hauled the trailer up to Robb's Well, loaded Blackberry, and returned to headquarters. Cole probed around in the wound and pulled out a piece of stick. He gave her an oral antibiotic and we returned her to Robb's Well. Each week, we checked on her. She seemed to be healing well until about week three, when the slightest of limps returned. By week four, all vestiges of Cole's surgery had disappeared and she was right back where she started—with an open, running sore and a full limp.

Cole said, "Maybe I better try again." This time he went deeper and shot antibiotics directly into the wound.

We watched her some more, but the infection wouldn't heal. She didn't complain. Every time I visited her, she acknowledged me with a whinny, friendly as ever. I'd ask her how she was doing and love on her, then she'd escort me to the gate and say goodbye. Just being around her set my day right. For six months, she had that infection, but never bad enough to warrant a call to the vet. The main side effect seemed to be that it stunted her growth. All the other horses had gained weight and stature. Not Blackberry. The infection consumed her energy and kept her short and kind of squat.

The next time Cole and I checked on Blackberry, we noticed her wound wasn't any better, but wasn't any worse either.

"Al, I think you need to sell her," Cole said. The thought had crossed my mind, but I had not grabbed hold of it. "She won't heal up. I'm afraid she'll never make a horse."

"I know. But I hate to lose any horse, especially one that's so good-natured," I said. Cole reminded me that the wound had changed her physically and might have changed her emotionally, too. I still saw a sweet, gentle horse, one of the sweetest I'd ever seen. "Look," I said, "I'm just not ready to give up on her. I know you've operated, but why don't we try once more? Open the wound with the scalpel and go a little deeper. Whad'ya say?"

Cole said okay. When he went in, he found a hole as big as his finger. He widened it and went deeper, removing infected tissue. We put in a bunch of antibiotics, gave her some combiotic shots to help stop the infection, let her rest in the corral for a week, then hauled her back to Robb's Well. The wound never reopened and Blackberry fully recovered. Except for a scar on her shoulder where Cole had whacked and cut on her. We turned her out for another year. By the time we hauled her in, she was a healthy, fat little girl.

Even though she was still small, I started riding her. She wasn't big enough to take out on really heavy days. If by chance she did have a long day, her strength would be zapped and she would need a good solid rest for a few days. No matter. She loved being around people and always wanted to know what was going on. When I went to catch a horse, her head popped up in hopes she would be the one I'd pick. On days I did choose her, she was eager to experience whatever I had in mind. We'd ride out and I'd share the day's itinerary and she'd walk and bob her head, agreeable to it all. On those days, I felt like I was hanging out with one of my best friends. Even if I was working alone gathering cattle, I never felt alone.

She never offered to buck except once. That was the day my daughter Marina didn't have a horse to ride.

"Why don't you ride Blackberry?" I said. "You'll love her." I saddled her up and Marina got on her. I forgot to tell her to hold up the reins a little and ride her off gently. That was my habit, my way of telling Blackberry I was there. I'd hold her up a little bit, ride a couple of yards, then let her have her head and all would be fine. Poor Marina didn't know that. Marina rode her down to the far end of the corral, where Blackberry put her head down and started to bow her back. "Hold her head up! Hold her head up!" I shouted. Whether Marina didn't hear me or chose not to follow my orders, I didn't know. But the next moment, Blackberry stuck her head between her legs and bucked about three jumps. Or at least it was her attempt at bucking. It looked more like crow hopping. Marina fell off. I went running over, already feeling bad because I hadn't given her the heads-up on what to do, but Marina realized what had happened. She didn't blame Blackberry. (She had every right to blame her father but didn't do that either.) She climbed back in the saddle and ended up making a new friend that day.

Around the time Blackberry turned ten, I hired a young cowboy for the roundup. He wanted to bring his own horse. Normally, the cowboys rode Lazy B horses. In fact, with the exception of those owned by some of my close friends, few outside horses ever came to the ranch. Our herd was so isolated that the horses didn't develop the antibodies for common diseases.

"Has your horse been sick recently or ever had any health problems?" I asked the cowboy.

"Oh no. Not at all. He's the healthiest old horse I've known. Helluva good rope horse, too."

A little voice nagged not to allow the horse in, but I didn't listen. "Well okay then. You can bring him."

When he arrived, that horse was starting to get sick with a kind of influenza that affects horses in their lungs, making it hard to breathe and causing a high fever. The symptoms were not yet evident. Within twenty-four hours, our entire remuda was sick—every horse, even the ones we didn't ride that day. All from that stupid horse I allowed to come on the ranch. When the horses' fevers shot up to 104 and 105 degrees, I was frightened that we would lose them and, on top of it, not get the cattle rounded up in time to sell. I called the vet and he came over and said, sure enough, this is influenza. He administered antibiotics and vaccines to the tune of twenty-five hundred bucks.

"You'll have to close down the roundup for a few weeks," he said, "while this thing runs its course. Keep them on good feed and don't ride them."

The horses we had been riding that day ran the highest fevers and became the sickest. It was one of the days I had chosen to ride Blackberry. The infection damaged her lungs to such a degree that after she recovered, she could gallop only about a hundred yards before she pulled up, panting and out of air. Previously, despite her small size, she could gallop quite a long way. For all practical purposes, we couldn't use her anymore, especially for roundups, when you're forced at times to gallop a lot farther than one hundred yards. I felt so sorry for Blackberry. She had such a sweet heart and had been through enough in her life.

I couldn't sell her, nor did I want to. Then it came to me what I could do with her. Our cook Janice Chote had a seven-year-old son who loved to hang around with the cowboys and wanted to be one ever so badly. When she wasn't cooking for our roundup, Janice lived in her home near Animas, New Mexico. She had a little five-acre patch of hay right next to her house. A perfect place for a horse. And one that came with a playmate who wanted nothing more than to be a cowboy with his own horse. So Blackberry went to live with Kyle Chote in New Mexico.

"Now you treat her gently, because she can't gallop around," I said, handing over the reins. "But you can ride her in a walk or a trot as much as you want." Talk about a boy being beyond ecstatic. I could tell he would love Blackberry beyond life itself.

Every so often I had reason to go to Animas, and the route brought me past the Chote homestead. If it was a weekend or a weekday after school let out, Kyle and Blackberry would be out in the hay field. Most of the time, he didn't have a bridle or saddle on Blackberry but would be on her bareback. She was a fat little girl with a kind of flat back. Kyle would lie on her back with his head by her hips, looking up at the clouds and the sky while his best friend grazed happily on hay.

I always felt bad Blackberry got that infection, but she sure did end up having a nice retirement. And for that, I was grateful.

CHAPTER TWELVE

Bound for Summer Grazing

The pinkness of dawn peeking around the edge of the blinds spoke of a clear day. Judging by the smell of bacon and coffee, it probably was time to get up. I must have fallen sound asleep around 4:00 a.m., the last time I checked the clock. Sleep had been fitful. Scenarios of the day's impending adventure kept playing out on the silver screen of my mind. In one version, I led a mile-long string of wild mustangs along spring-green rolling country, brought them through gates, and without a hitch delivered them to the promised pasture of Mud Lake. The cowboys and horses all did their jobs. It was a blockbuster of a success. In the next screenplay, our entourage hit the three-mile point when something spooked a group of horses. They took off running perpendicular to the herd. Their draft sucked up horses behind them. The cowboys lost control and hundreds of mustangs scattered across the ranch, jumping fences, repudiating our long hours of training. That image kept rewinding and replaying.

I pulled up the blind. With noisy ceremony, a wild turkey flapped down from its nighttime perch in the big elm and bobbled toward the group already en route to the pond. It was May tenth. The day needed to go as beautifully as the sun sparkling on the water.

How could the horses not stay together? We had spent so much time with them they practically had graduate degrees in following a man on horseback. These horses were wild, but still they were horses as much as Aunt Jemima, Blackberry, and Saber. They had heart and soul. I believed we had touched that part of them where trust and loyalty reside and the bonds of friendship form. The preliminary tests—vaccinating the entire herd in less than a day, moving them through corrals and lanes and into various pastures—indicated that today's move to Mud Lake would end on a successful note. If it didn't, well, I would need a new game plan on how to run the sanctuary.

I dressed and went out to the kitchen. Alan Jr. stood at the stove frying eggs. He wouldn't have missed this day for the world. My friend Ralph Stinson, a retired physician, highly medaled World War II pilot, and all-around good guy, had flown out from California to join us. An investor in the sanctuary, he had fallen in love with the ranch during a visit the previous fall. When I told him we would be taking the horses out to summer grazing, he asked if he could join in. He had arrived a few days ago with enthusiasm and optimism that infused my own.

Alan Jr. whisked my plate away as I chewed the last bite of breakfast and had the kitchen cleaned before Ralph and I finished our coffee. His usual calm demeanor was on fast forward this morning. We headed across the dewy grass to John's house. I wondered if the horses out in the distant pasture were stirring, picking up on the energy of our pumping adrenaline. The screen door of the big house swung open and Megan bounded down the porch steps.

"Daddy said it's moving day for the horses, Alan." She grabbed my hand. "Do you think if I sit real quiet on Clyde I could come with you?"

I scooped her up. "Tell you what, sweetheart. Those horses will need some loving when they're all settled in their summer home. We'll saddle up Clyde and you can help make a hand then. How'd that be?"

After a three-second pout, Megan bobbed her ponytail. "Okay. Maybe tomorrow, huh?"

I laughed, the tension in my jaw siphoning off. "Maybe tomorrow," I said. I carried her up the stairs and set her down with a tickle in the mudroom. I tossed my hat on the bench and led the way into the kitchen. John and Jordan sat at the table, the map of the ranch spread out between them. Jordan had shaken off his teenage sluggishness at the prospect of missing school and looked alert as he wolfed down a donut. Russ and Marty leaned over, following John's finger along the map.

John looked up. "Mornin' everyone. Grab yourselves some coffee and donuts." Debbie restocked the empty plate in front of Jordan.

Here we were, the magnificent seven, or at least the seven, magnificent if we could pull off our adventure. Between us, we had over a century of experience working with horses. I filled a coffee mug and sat down for the last-minute cram session that we didn't really need but felt reassured doing.

"You all know the plan. John and I are going to lead." We had figured the two of us could best hold the pace to an easy gallop even with the lead horses pushing us to go faster. If horses accelerate to full speed, they tend to lose touch with reality and slip into full fright-and-flight mode. If that happened, regaining control would be about as likely as preventing the sun from setting. We'd have to head back home and try again another day when panic wasn't their strongest emotion.

"We'll gather them just before this corner," I said, pointing to the space on the map, "and get them warmed up with a training drive around the pasture. When we get to the northwest corner, we'll go out the gate. Then it's on to Mud Lake." I looked around the group to make sure everyone understood.

"Russ and Marty, you two will bring up the rear. Alan Jr. and Jordan, once we take them through the first gate you each take a side and keep the herd from getting too wide." The only one remaining was Ralph. "You tag along in the Suburban," I said to him.

We rehashed the issue of the babies. This had been a concern for weeks now. Would they be able to keep up at the fast pace for six miles? The oldest was no more than fifty days and the youngest had been born only two days ago. How would these gangly, long-legged foals keep up with their mothers? No one could answer that question. Even though we had spent the past four months planning for this, mulling over the possibilities and options, we couldn't account for every little detail. Such is life on a ranch. Sometimes it's like improv theater. You make up the lines as you go.

Debbie and Megan's chorus of good luck followed us out of the kitchen. I settled my hat and inhaled the crisp, fresh air. The lawn had spruced up its green carpet in honor of the day. Even the barn with its fresh coat of red paint and midwestern charm seemed to herald our presence. We stepped into our man cave and our horses stirred in greeting. Clyde cocked an ear when he saw me. "Hey Clyde," I said. "Were you wondering about breakfast?" I spread out the sweet-smelling grain mixture in his manger. A shaft of sunlight illuminated fine dust drifting above his bent head. While he munched, I curried him and listened to the clinks of cowboy gear and the banter of cowboys.

"Get off my foot," Jordan yelled at his horse.

"Am I goin' to have to saddle that horse for you?" said Russ.

"Hell, no. He's just being a butthead."

I hefted my saddle over Clyde's back and felt the immediate connection that always ensued. My twenty-year-old saddle had been made to my specifications by Wilbur Thomas. The leather was half-worn, but I had no intention of replacing it. Every cowboy becomes attached to his personal saddle, and every saddle feels different. This one was a gem. Clyde wiggled under its weight and, smart as ever, held his breath while I cinched him.

I patted his rump and led him out into the training arena. "This is it, buddy. The big day we've been working on. You'll do great. Look at the shape you've gotten into." I rubbed his neck. "You just be your calm, cool self and we'll do fine." I pulled the cinch one notch tighter and swung into the saddle for what would be one of the most defining rides of my cowboying career.

We rode through the corrals into the wide lane leading to the heifer pasture and the wild horses. I heard the distant rumble of the Suburban. Ralph planned to keep us in sight but stay a respectable distance behind so as not to alarm the horses. They knew the truck, of course, but the day would be so out of their routine that even a familiar truck doing the unfamiliar—traveling at a faster speed than normal and pushing from behind—might add to the anxiety they were sure to feel.

Russ dismounted and opened the gate into the pasture. We rode through at an easy trot and headed up the grassy hill. At the top, a prairie panorama stretched out before us. Without anyone saying a word, we stopped. It happened every time. It was like being parched and coming to a well with fresh, cold water. I gulped in the sight. Miles and miles of grass waved at us, happy to be speckled with twelve hundred wild horses.

"Okay boys," I said. "Here we go."

The horses' trademark scent reached us first. That strong, pungent smell of wildness sweating through the pores of their skin. When they saw us coming, they shook their heads and threw snorts that drifted toward us on the light breeze. We were familiar to them, but each time we met, an innate nervousness overpowered them. Seven of us spreading across the pasture told them that some drama was about to unfold and they were not to be mere bystanders. They stomped and called for each other. They started to move into one large herd, as if convening to discuss the situation. The soprano whinnies of the colts and fillies sat high in the air; under them came mamas with nuzzles of reassurance and an offer of milk.

I looked down the line of riders, checking our formation. With measured pace, we swept around the south side of the pasture. The leaders of the herd felt the gentle pressure and moved out

10. Horses galloping toward Mud Lake

along the fence heading north, then hit the corner and headed east. As the leaders picked up speed, John and I peeled away from the line and galloped in front of them to set the pace. We rode side by side about twenty feet apart, with maybe twenty or thirty lead horses close behind us, so close we could hear their rhythmic breathing. A peloton of mustangs ran behind them. We all settled into a comfortable gallop. Like a thick rope uncoiling, the herd began to string out and lengthen, with most of the mamas and babies at the back. The forty-eight hundred hooves beating the sand sounded like the muted thunder of Indian drums. The sound reverberated in the ground, up through Clyde and my saddle, and into my bloodstream. My entire being thrilled to the awe of the moment. Even then, I knew it was the pinnacle ride of my ranching career.

John and I continually turned to view the action behind us, keeping our eye on it. So far, all the players were in position. Then, without provocation, a big brown gelding and a bay veered out of the herd. As if prompted by some premeditated, hidden signal, they turned in unison ninety degrees, pinned their ears back, and shifted into high gear. They started running toward Alan Jr. and his horse, riding fifty feet away. Al noticed them, but no alarm registered in his posture. I wasn't alarmed either. Few cowboys I know have been attacked by horses that turned out of a group. But darn, if those horses didn't keep running. They were in attack mode. Before I could yell a warning, they slammed their chests at the same instant into the side of Al's mount. The unsuspecting horse hit the ground flat on her side. A large grunt, audible above the galloping herd, whooshed out of her and her legs continued to run through the air like she was trying to escape the vicious attackers. Alan flew through the air. He plowed a face-plant furrow in the sand ten feet beyond his horse, thankfully away from the running herd. He lay there stone still.

Every parent totes a box of pure terror, the latch of which springs open only if your child is seriously injured or, God forbid, killed. In that instant, the latch on my black box released and out poured thick, heart-stopping darkness. I turned Clyde, raced toward my son, and jumped off before the horse stopped.

I dropped to my knees. "Alan!" I yelled close to his ear. I was afraid to move him for fear something had broken. I scanned his arms and legs. Nothing seemed to be at an odd angle. I was about to feel for a pulse when I saw his fingers wiggle. The movement shoved part of the terror back in its box.

At that moment, John rode up. His face reflected the horror still gripping me. "He's unconscious," I said. I looked up to see where Ralph was. The Suburban was on a hill in the distance, turning toward us. I noticed Alan's horse stand up and give herself a good shake. The other cowboys rode up. One of Alan's legs twitched. I prayed that was a good sign and not a harbinger of injury.

John and I rolled Al over. His face looked like a mask of sand. I cleaned the sand out of his nostrils. His eyes fluttered, and I quickly brushed the sand from them. He probably had sand down his shirt and pants and even in his boots. He peered through glazed eyes as if trying to comprehend what life-form we were.

"How many fingers am I holding up?" I said.

Al frowned and tried to push himself up. I cleaned out his ears and repeated the question. "Three," Al said, sounding like someone who drank one too many shots of tequila.

John and I started asking questions. Does anything hurt? Can you focus? What day of the week is it? My son answered while clumsily brushing himself off. He extended a hand and we helped him up.

He looked around and in true cowboy fashion said, "Where's my horse? We've gotta get going."

"Hold on there, partner," I said. His eyes still had a film of fog. The Suburban pulled up and Ralph hopped out.

"You really got your bell rung, didn't you?" he said to Alan, already starting to take his pulse. He examined the rest of him and said, "Nothing broken, though you might have a concussion."

"Does he need to be in the hospital?" I asked.

"Dad, no. I'll be fine. If we get going, we'll be done by noon."

"What do you think?" I asked Ralph.

"You can take the safe route and go to the hospital." Ralph frowned in contemplation. "Or not."

I could see where this was going. If I had done the face plant and could get up and walk, I would be saying the same thing as my son. What every family needs—two stupid, hardheaded cowboys. I looked at the horses now scattered around the pasture. The day had done a face plant. Maybe we didn't know enough about these horses. They had been following us beautifully. What could have triggered those two ornery animals to charge? We'd never be able to answer that question.

The logical side of me said to call it a day, take my boy to the hospital, get him checked out, return to the ranch, and regroup. At the same time, a different voice yapped in my other ear. Stay. Finish the job. Al is banged up good, but he and his horse are okay.

11. Horses passing through a gate on their way to summer grazing

Trust me, like you have all the other times. I recognized that voice, the one that had said let Aunt Jemima chase the runaway steer, the one that said don't give up on Blackberry, the one that had urged me to buy the ranch and lobby the government to support a wild horse sanctuary.

I looked at Alan. "You sure you're up to this?"

"Let's go." He took the reins of his horse from Russ.

We had a board meeting right there. We decided that those two horses knew exactly what they were doing and should they or others reenact the attack, we'd take their advances seriously and get the hell out of the way. I didn't understand how those horses had communicated to turn at the same instant. They had been in exact lockstep. Had they been out in the pasture practicing this move when we weren't around?

The horses gathered easily. John and I moved out front again, leading the horses around the pasture, this time counterclockwise. I didn't want to mimic what we had done before and the only variable that could be changed was direction. They hit an easy gallop. When we neared the west gate, John picked up the pace so he could open the gate into the Big Horse pasture. I felt pretty sure the lead horses would follow me through, but still my breath caught as I rode between the gateposts. The horses behind me threaded through like they'd done it a hundred times before.

We continued without incident across the three-mile pasture. Over a little hill lay the gate leading into the West Whitelands pasture, which was two and a half miles from Mud Lake. John opened the gate and the horses never slowed. On they went. Too fast, as it turned out. Clyde's gait changed ever so slightly, indicating his gallop required more effort. I motioned for John to keep going and slowed down. I didn't want Clyde to run down. I pulled to the side and trotted as the leaders galloped by. I thought of Saber—big, athletic, able to travel long distances. He would have been the perfect horse to ride on this venture. I pictured him gliding over the sandy country. I spent but a moment with him, then tucked him away. I was needed here and now.

I looked back. A chestnut mare had turned and for a second I thought she was going to bolt from the herd, but she ran to check on her foal. Ah, it was the mama of the gangly-legged, youngest baby that was having a hard time keeping up with the herd. Mama pushed him from behind. He put his head down and tried to run a little faster but couldn't quite get there. Mama ran ahead of him searching for help. Not finding any she returned to her baby. Ralph noticed the colt and decided to help by honking the horn. The harsh blares blew above the soft thunder of hooves. Despite his best intentions, his honking was spooking the horses. The leaders picked up the pace. The edge of pandemonium started to encroach. Russ was riding closest to the colt. I broke from my position and rode back to him.

I pointed to the colt. "Go catch him," I yelled to Russ. "He's not going to make it. Use your saddle rope to tie him in the back of the Suburban." Russ nodded and veered toward the struggling baby. I pointed Clyde west again toward Mud Lake. Al Jr. rode ahead of me and didn't appear to be under any stress. We still had at least a half mile to go.

Clyde slowed some more. With John, Marty, Alan Jr., and Jordan up front and handling everything well, I fell back, letting Clyde choose a comfortable gait. The Suburban grumbled behind me. I looked back to see where it was and almost fell out of my saddle. Ralph, still in the driver's seat, had acquired a most unusual passenger. Russ must not have tied the colt down, and somehow the little guy had climbed from the back of the truck to the front and plopped in the front passenger seat. He looked like a Great Dane with both legs on the dash and licking the windshield. In front of the vehicle, his mother raced back and forth, frantic to get her baby back. The baby stopped licking and parted his teeth. He probably nickered for his mama, and she sure as heck heard it. She turned toward the Suburban, flattened her ears, and charged. Ralph watched in horror. He couldn't back up or turn, so he stopped. Just before she ran into the hood, she spun around in a cloud of dust and kicked out the front grille. Ralphs's mouth dropped open as she vented her fury on the metal. The colt looked like a little kid cheering his parent. My mouth dropped open, too, a belly laugh bursting out at the sight of the big colt next to the ace bomber pilot who sat there wide-eyed. Oh, for a camera. Frustrated, Mama ran off to catch up to the rest of the herd. Nothing could be done about her tantrum right now. We'd resolve the issue at Mud Lake.

By this time, the lead horses were half a mile ahead and had started to flow through the gate into Mud Lake pasture. John, still on horseback, stood beyond the gate and off to the side watching. With no lead man to follow, the herd fanned out. The other men's horses began to fade. The pace we had kept was too fast for the saddle horses to maintain. No one had anticipated this happening.

Clyde and I were the last horse and cowboy to ride through. The Suburban followed with the colt still in the passenger seat

12. A colt trying to keep up with his mama

and Mama running back and forth next to the moving vehicle. Ralph pulled to a stop. I dismounted and walked over to the truck. When I opened the door, the colt twisted and turned until one skinny foreleg flopped out, then out popped a head with searching eyes. Since his mother was practically breathing down my neck, I helped the little guy out. He stumbled for a few steps, but Mama propped him up with nuzzles and offered a good long drink of milk. The look she gave Ralph clearly indicated she didn't want him as a babysitter ever again.

The horses seemed pleased to find an abundance of tender, sweet grass. Happy stood at the outskirts of the herd, his neck curved toward the ground. The palomino twins grazed near the middle, the family of roans nearby. I recognized other individual horses here and there. All had made the journey successfully. The breeze blowing against my back delivered a sense of accomplishment. It eased through me, softening the disappointment that I had been feeling over the wreck and our horses tiring. I had never imagined either of these things happening. I reminded myself that everyone

13. Horses galloping across the prairie

arrived here in one piece and the horses had followed the leader for six miles. I joined the cowboys unsaddling in the old corral.

"Load up, boys, the bus is here," Ralph said. Seven magnificent cowboys, one emptying the sand out of his boots, piled in. We all had a story to tell. Over ham and cheese sandwiches in the Pitkins' kitchen, I related Ralph's little adventure, which set everyone to laughing so hard they could barely eat. It was destined to become part of ranch lore. There was a consensus that in the future motorcycles would come in handy for long treks. No one said, or even insinuated, the wreck had tarnished our once-in-a-lifetime day.

That night I crawled into bed exhausted and fell asleep to the sound of hooves pounding the sandy soil and a vision of tails and manes waving free and easy in the wind.

CHAPTER THIRTEEN

Saber

The new colt in the corral at Lazy B headquarters caught my eye. The cowboys had brought him, his mama, and the eight other mares and ten-month-old foals in from the pasture where they had been born. It was weaning day. It took an hour to separate mamas and babies. The mares took a last, long, loving look at their foals and with a goodbye nuzzle headed back on their own volition to the pasture for grazing. Since they were only a few months away from the birth of their next babies, their bodies were telling them it was time to wean the current foals. The colts didn't have a chance to mourn their departed mothers; they had to start school. The curriculum included learning to lead, learning to load in a trailer on command, and learning to trust the two-legged creatures who were now picking their feet up and asking them to stand still. We rewarded them with the new taste of grain.

This particular colt had a larger build than his peers, with a broad chest, smooth barrel, and muscular hips. The dark hair that most foals have at birth had been replaced with a shiny white coat, a dark stocking above each hoof, a black mane, and a streak of black down his backbone reminiscent of Spanish influence. He explored his new territory, poking along the fence, his nose up and ears forward, and when the cowboys weren't holding class, nudged his more timid companions into games. He was the leader on the playground, and he brought home a report card full of As, though sometimes the teacher had to work at keeping his attention, which drifted if he learned the lesson quickly and became bored.

I felt an instant attraction similar to what you feel when you meet someone you want to get to know better. Maybe it's the energy in the smile and eyes or the sweep of hands in conversation, or you see a glimmer of something that reminds you of yourself and you know that you want to start spending more time with that person. This little white guy fit those characteristics. I could see him in my string of horses. It wasn't a decision I needed to make right then since he was headed out to Robb's Well for the next fifteen months or so.

When I was in the area of Robb's Well, I would stop to see the young horses. I observed how they walked and how much they had grown. I also did a sort of mental check-in to see if it was time to integrate them into the ranch system. Which horses in our strings would soon be retired? How many hands were available to bring them in and break them? When we had the extra hands I'd send out a few cowboys to round up the horses at Robb's Well, cut five or six of the biggest ones, and bring them into headquarters for breaking.

I had been keeping an eye on the white horse. The day he arrived at the corral, I was waiting for him. Though he had not yet attained full stature, the muscles in his upper legs, forelegs, and haunches had thickened, and the vertical between his belly and the ground had lengthened. He had a smooth, effortless gait that exuded confidence. Based on his physique, coordination, and disposition, I already could tell the white horse had the potential to be an athlete. I could see the disappointment on the cowboys' faces when I said, "I'll take that white one for my string."

He needed a better name than "that white horse." The best way to name a horse is to allow the name to emerge. It always does. Once, as teenager, I named a horse Dumas. My dad and I attended the 1956 Olympic trials at the Los Angeles Coliseum, and we saw Charles Dumas set the world record by clearing seven feet in the high jump. Shortly after, one of our young horses went and jumped a six-foot-high corral and I promptly named him Dumas. Aunt Jemima found her name when a can of syrup stuck to her foot. And her mother, Tequila, well, we don't need to go there.

The white horse reminded me of Robert E. Lee's famed white horse Traveller. I recalled seeing some photos of Lee mounted on this steed, dressed in full military regalia with a saber hanging at his side. Saber. Now there was a strong, steadfast word. "Hey you rascal," I said to him one morning, my arm extended over the fence into his space. He trotted over for a pet. "You good with the name Saber? I'm thinking you can live up to it. What do you think?" He pushed his nose against my shoulder.

Saber and I began to get acquainted. Since he wasn't full-grown, and probably wouldn't be for another year, he couldn't do a hard day's work, but he could join me on less demanding days. Saber had an idea of what he wanted, and what he wanted didn't always agree with my bidding. Sometimes he could get a little prickly. He never bucked, but he didn't always want to cooperate. If I wanted him to turn right, he pulled to go left. If I rode him with spurs and touched him, and I rarely touched him, he'd look back and kick a hind foot at the spurs or try to bite them, an especially annoying habit. By this point in my life, I had moved away from the Jim Brister style of breaking a horse by breaking his will. Too often this required punishing a horse severely and I had grown unwilling to settle for the consequences. Candy had drowned and Sally's entire personality changed. I had vowed to break Saber in a more gentle fashion. Except this required dredging for patience because Saber could be like a burr in my boot.

One day we were driving cattle back from New Well to the Lazy B headquarters, a six-mile trip. The previous two days of rounding up had been difficult, dusty work, but this was an easy day so I opted to ride Saber. Jim Brister was pointing the cattle up front with another cowboy. The herd fanned out behind them. I brought up the drag in the back with the rest of the cowboys to show that I wasn't above doing drudgery work. I could see the whole show from there and could tell who was or wasn't carrying his load. Maybe Saber wanted to be in the lead or maybe he was bored. Whatever the issue, he was crankier than a teenager awakened from a sound sleep. I'd spur him along and he'd turn and try to bite me. It seemed like every hundred feet I was pulling his head up and scolding him. I was getting annoyed at him being annoyed at me. That's when I saw Jim break from the lead and circle back toward me, something he wouldn't do unless he had to unload a piece of his mind.

He rode up next to me and gave Saber the once-over. "Alan, if I were on that damn horse, I'd draw that knot in your get-down rope and whip that thing against his sheath until he squealed for mercy." I held back a wince. The sheath protects a horse's penis and is a very sensitive area.

Saber's strong shoulders shifted rhythmically under my saddle and a cow in front of us called out for her calf. I didn't want to argue with Jim or go against his judgment. I may have been the boss, but Jim was my senior and my mentor. For the first time in my life, I bucked his opinion. "Well, I'm trying something a little different on him this time. I'm going to give him a chance to learn it on his own," I said.

Saber turned his head and jabbed his mouth at my spurs. Large teeth flashed between curled lips. I yanked the reins, pulling his head back. Jim looked straight ahead and without a word rode off.

"Damn it, Saber. Knock it off. What are you thinking?"

Saber jogged a few side steps. I took a deep breath. It was going to be a long day.

Not every day with Saber was long, and of course I didn't ride him every day. Occasionally he would be so interested in the task at hand that neither of us remembered that I wore spurs. Within a few hours, however, he would bicker with me, forcing me to ladle out more patience and reaffirm my vow of training. I could see his potential when I watched him in the corral, feel it when we galloped, trotted, or even walked. He was long-legged, powerfully so, and could outrun his peers. I never timed him or any horse, but if I had I suspect he would have won the race by many lengths. I babied him with extra grain, and like a teenage boy inhaling any food put in front of him, he continued to grow.

As he learned cowboying, I learned gentle horse training. Most cowboys forced a horse right there and then to submit to their will. Within a day or two, the horse wouldn't have an ounce of argument left. More often than not, when Saber returned to the horse pasture for the night and I slid off my boots and hung my hat, issues between us remained unresolved.

About three months after Jim offered his advice, something happened. It was an unassuming day. Saber and I led a crew of cowboys to cut out cattle for sale. The sun spilled over us, bright as always, and a mischievous breeze scrambled the desert dust with the thuds of hard hooves and the sweat of men on horseback. We were nearing a late lunch when it hit me. On any other day, Saber would have tested me a dozen times by now. But here he was with his head and ears held high, so fully engaged in his job that I hadn't needed to reprimand or spur him once all morning. In fact, he had just moved a large steer to the outside of the herd with little direction from me. I had eyed the steer and thought, okay, this guy needs to go. Maybe my hands had slightly, perhaps subconsciously, pulled the reins in the steer's direction, but maybe not. Maybe Saber read my mind. Regardless, he had moved the animal, slowly, gently, and before I knew it, had the steer in exactly the right spot at the edge of the herd. A new alertness tensed his body. I could feel us working together.

I said, "Wow, Saber, you've arrived." It was like what a hunter experiences the first time his young dog points, waits for the shot, then perfectly retrieves the bird. By the time we returned to headquarters, I was sitting on a completely different horse. For whatever reason, Saber's resistance had hopped off the train and full cooperation had moved in. From that day on, Saber became the best cow horse I ever rode. When we were out on the range, he seemed to know what I wanted to do. It was as if this athletic, smart companion could read my mind. I'd throw the saddle over him, chitchatting about the day like you would chat to your best friend, and then we would have the luxury of spending the entire day together, hanging out, running into challenges, having adventures. The line between work and pleasure dissolved.

About the same time, Saber did another extraordinary thing I've never seen a horse repeat. One morning, the air cool against our faces, we set out at Saber's usual gait. I urged him to walk a little faster. I felt his gait change. He had broken into a running walk, the same gait as a Tennessee walking horse. No other horse on the ranch had such a gait, so he hadn't learned by imitating. His body naturally slipped into the pattern. I didn't even know how to respond except to enjoy the ride. It was like stepping off a tractor and into a Lexus.

"What the hell got into your horse? He just hit fourth gear. How'd you teach him that?" said Cole, pulling up beside me. His horse had to hit a long trot to keep up with Saber.

I shrugged my shoulders. "Good cowboys get the best out of their horses," I said. Three miles later Saber wasn't even out of breath. The boss always sets the pace when riding out to the roundup and cowboy culture says you never gripe about that pace. But that day the crew certainly looked disgruntled.

Another time, on an early fall day, the cattle were scattered on the High Lonesome pasture in the Summit section of Lazy B, a half-day horse ride from headquarters. I gathered a crew of cowboys and, to save time, we loaded our horses in trailers and drove out to Summit. Saber was still young, a green colt that could handle a day of rounding up cattle spread out over the six square miles of pasture.

The grass at High Lonesome grew the thickest on the ranch. It didn't have to angle around mesquite trees or contort between rocks. It just had to poke its head straight through the soft ground and drink the sunshine. Only an occasional badger hole dotted the ground.

I assigned each cowboy an area of pasture. We had just started to spread out when a coyote jumped up right in front of Saber and me. Its gray, mangy body tripped my cowboy switch and I plunged right into roping mode. Cowboys are trained practically at birth to go after anything running away from them—rabbits, bobcats, calves, coyotes. It's not that you need to catch the animal. It's the challenge of the event. Are you good enough to rope the critter? If you do, you've earned your bragging rights.

I turned Saber on that coyote. He knew exactly what we were up to and caught up to the coyote like he was standing still. I jerked my rope down and built a loop. I leaned forward to throw the loop, and BAM, Saber stepped in a badger hole. His front end jolted down. His back end popped up. We were going so fast I didn't have a split second to lean back and regain my balance. The sudden stop shot me over Saber's neck, ass over teakettle into the air right toward that running coyote. The only thing going through my harebrained mind was, oh shit, this really is going to hurt. And it did.

I rolled to a crumpled stop and lifted my head, looking for Saber to see if he had broken a leg. He was getting up from his fall, twenty feet away, and had a terrified look in his eyes. He didn't even shake himself but took off running, a white streak across the brown desert. Aw hell, is about all I could think. Well, at least he ran without a limp. I pulled myself up, my rope still in hand, and hobbled across the hard ground after my hat, cussing myself out for being such a stupid cowboy to rise to this bait. I surveyed my distant crew. You would think by the way their horses' rear ends faced me they hadn't seen my dumbass attack. But I knew they had. Feeling the fool, I began limping along the two-and-a-half-mile trek across the pasture to reclaim my horse. He wouldn't be able to go beyond the fence, but would he be able to forgive me? If I hadn't been on Saber, I never would have tried to rope that coyote. No other horse could have caught him.

An hour later, a few cowboys started heading toward me, Saber in tow.

"Gee, boss, what happened?" Snicker.

"You know what happened. Don't you be laughing at me. You all have had a fall before."

I took the reins. "Saber, can you forgive my stupidity? I shouldn't have turned you to that coyote. I'll try to be a better friend to you from here on. I owe you one." I climbed back in the saddle. And Saber? Friend that he was, he went on like nothing had happened.

By the time Saber was five, he was so powerful and fast that when we worked cattle I always held him back a little. One day, curiosity got the better of me. I finished lunch before anyone else at the bunkhouse and didn't feel like shooting the breeze, so I headed outside to get a jump on re-saddling Saber. He was feeding with the other horses in the corral by the barn. That morning we had herded four hundred cows and another two hundred calves into the large working lot at headquarters, where we would spend the afternoon selecting and cutting cow-and-calf pairs. Calves over six months would be sold; younger calves would be branded and remain on the ranch.

I put my hand on Saber's neck and led him over to the saddle I had set on the ground. He looked like he was as eager to get out of the corral as I had been to get out of the bunkhouse. I could feel his muscles under my hand, relaxed but alert, ready for action. I saddled up and settled on the worn leather like you settle in a car seat. But this wasn't a minivan or pickup or souped-up SUV. This wasn't a Lexus or Infiniti or even a BMW or Mercedes.

This was a Ferrari.

I had never done an all-out test drive. Every day I obeyed the speed limits. What would it feel like to pull on the Autobahn, shift into eighth gear, and let it go? It would be plain wrong never to answer that question. It was time to see how truly fast my horse could run.

I walked Saber through the empty corrals and into the working lot. The cattle had drifted into siesta mode, bunched in one end of the long corral. I spotted a big, old Brahman cow that I knew was fast.

"Let's give this gal a chase, Saber." I was the racecar driver at the starting line, the F-16 fighter pilot about to break the sound barrier for the first time. Adrenaline and curiosity revved my blood.

Saber knew what to do. He pushed that cow out of the bunch toward the back of the corral, close to the fence fortified with rows of double barbed wire. She swung her head back and forth, irritated at having to move. Saber jump-started her into a sprint and took off after her. I let the reins go slack, shifting him right into eighth gear. He passed that cow like she was moving in slow motion, pulled ahead of her to turn her back against the fence. He pivoted so hard we angled to the ground, like a water-skier taking a quick turn, elbow and shoulder skimming the water. My lower leg dragged on the ground. Before I knew it, we were sliding across the soft ground, rocketing toward the barbed wire instead of along it. My leg was tucked under Saber's side, and I was still in the saddle. The sandpaper ground roughed my arm and side. The barbed wire rose toward us like the wall of a racetrack rising toward the driver of an out-of-control car. But where a driver has only the traction of a slick track, we had the traction of soft earth. It slowed us down like sand and gravel slow a runaway truck.

We came to a complete stop. I was in the saddle, but on my side, one leg under Saber and one on top. Other than Saber's weight compressing my trapped leg, nothing hurt. I lifted my head and assessed our predicament. Saber's legs had slid under the barbed wire, but he had miraculously stopped just before his belly made contact with it. But I could see the surly wire inches above him, ready to attack at his slightest move and tear into him. The fear that he would try to scramble up gripped me.

"Saber, look, we're in a fix here," I said, trying to sound calmer than I felt. "It's not your fault your legs slid out from under you. I ran you too fast and turned you back too hard." I rubbed his neck. "I'm the one to blame here. But right now, I need you to lay here real quiet and not struggle, because if you struggle, you're going to hurt yourself."

I kept petting him and talking to him, assuring him the other cowboys would be out soon. Saber didn't move one muscle. He just lay there like he was going to take a nap in the sun. I didn't dare dislodge my leg from under him or sidle out of the saddle. If you go down together, you stay down together. Besides, I knew someone would be headed our way soon. Funny how "soon" can feel like the span between lunch and dinner.

Jim Brister arrived first on horseback. He looked down at us, assessing the situation. "Looks like you got yourself in a helluva wreck here, Al." He threw down one end of his rope, waited for me to put the loop around my saddle horn. He dallied the rope on his saddle horn and then turned his horse to pull Saber and me out from under the fence. We slid out as smoothly as a deck of cards falling out of a tilted box. Saber lifted his head, pushed his feet into the ground, and snorted. I swung my free leg over him and disengaged from the saddle as he hoisted himself up. Then I found my legs, brushed off the dirt stuck to my shirt, and readjusted my chaps and hat, still perched on my head. Saber pawed a hoof at the ground as if scolding it for betraying him.

"No, Saber," I said. "I own this one, buddy. Blame me."

I untied the rope and threw it back to Jim. I waited for the question to pop, the one that hung between us: What happened here? All Jim did was recoil the rope, hang it back on his saddle, and ride off. But under that black hat of his, I thought I saw the tiniest of smirks.

"If you're rounding up at Robb's Well, you oughta bring a gun. The biggest buck is running around up there." My friend Eddie's excitement palpitated through the phone. He loved hunting season and had a hunting permit on our ranch. I can take it or leave it, but his enthusiasm sparked that competitive edge in me. "You shoot him, hang him in the tree, and I'll come get him," he said. Well, that sealed the deal. I got down my rifle and cleaned it, so it would be ready at 3:00 a.m. when the crew and I headed out. I didn't even have to think twice about which horse I would take.

Sure enough, the next day while Saber and I were scouring for cattle in the remote part of the range down near Robb's Well, a king-sized buck popped out from behind a clump of greasewood fifty feet from us. He stood for a cautious second, a regal rack of antlers balanced between radar ears. His nose twitched with the scent of enemy. Then off he shot, crashing through the brush.

I had a split second to decide if we were good for the chase. Before I could utter a word, Saber burst into action. "We're gonna catch him, Saber," I yelled. I held the reins slack in my right hand and grabbed my rifle in the left. The buck bounded in front of us, tacking around mesquite, springing over rocks, another athlete in his prime. Saber hurtled forward, his hooves thundering against the hollow ground, gaining on the animal. I leaned into the rushing air. Twenty, fifteen, ten more yards and we'd be within shooting range.

"Whoa," I said. Saber slowed. I took aim. The barrel bobbed in time with Saber's panting. I couldn't steady it. There was no way I could get a shot off. The buck didn't wait.

"Saber," I said, lowering my rifle, "I hate to ask you to do this, but we've got to get him. This time I'll jump down to shoot." Saber hadn't taken his eyes off the racing deer. "Do you think you can catch him again?"

Saber lit out. That deer must have been surprised to hear hoof-beats gaining on him. Saber flew over rocks and brush like he was on an asphalt track running the sixty-yard dash. He ran within twenty-five yards of that deer. I stopped him, jumped off, took aim, and fired. Instead of crumpling to the ground, the deer bounded over a little gully and ran behind a tree, then a rock. I couldn't track him with the rifle. Goddamnit. My horse had performed and I had dropped the ball. I leaned against Saber and stomped my boot heel into the dirt. But I climbed back on. Saber had run quite a ways, at least a quarter mile, maybe even a half. He was panting but not gasping for air. Dare I ask?

"Saber, can you catch him one more time?"

The horse that never said no took off for the third time. Our last chance. I couldn't ask him to do this again. We ran up on that old buck so close I could have roped him. A big wash suddenly appeared, and the buck was running so fast that he couldn't stop and tumbled out of sight. Saber came to a screeching halt. I threw the reins down, hopped off with my rifle, and ran over to the edge. Ten feet below me the buck lay on his side. I took a deep breath, aimed, and pulled the trigger.

Saber and I strung that deer over a tree using my saddle rope, and the next day Eddie drove the truck out and collected him.

I always knew where Saber was on the ranch. He was my number-one horse and my best friend. Yes, I loved Aunt Jemima dearly. She had won my heart in her own special way. And I loved my other horses—Blackberry, Tequila. Love is not finite. We are creatures capable of loving many times over, loving all our children, all our friends, all our pets. But every relationship boasts its own set of fingerprints. My relationship with Saber glittered with adventures, but we shared life on a deeper level. If horses can be soul mates, Saber was mine.

When I walked across the pasture, still monotone in the dimness of dawn, to catch him, he gave me a look that told me he was glad to see me and was ready to work. When we herded cattle, I almost could see his mind in action, planning out the next, best play and then with that innate gift of athletic coordination, putting it into action. We thought alike when it came to ranching. We embraced new experiences. Best of all, we respected each other one hundred percent. With mutual respect came true companionship and the magical bond of being best friends.

By the time he was six years old, Saber had reached his prime. After about age sixteen, seventeen, maybe eighteen, we'd retire our horses from ranch work. Some of them went on to live until they were twenty or even twenty-five. I didn't put it past Saber to be working cattle into his third decade.

It was an early summer evening, when the sun sits a little longer in the sky. I had turned Saber out in the horse pasture and was at home in my office catching up on some bookkeeping before dinner.

My mother came into the room, her face ashen, tears streaming down her face. She had been driving the Chrysler, returning from town, and was on the part of the main ranch road that ran through the horse pasture for a half mile or so. When she rounded the bend, sunlight exploded in front of her, penetrating the protection of the lowered visor and her sunglasses, robbing her of vision. She didn't know which horse she hit until she got out of the car. There were five standing alongside the road, as they always were at that point in the pasture. One horse lay in the middle of the road. It was Saber. The impact broke his hind leg at the knee, the one place on a horse that can't heal.

One of my fast and hard rules is that I never ask someone to do something that I couldn't do myself. I have broken that rule

only once in my life. I asked Cole Webb to put Saber down. I had
put down his favorite dog some years back. I would not have been
able to hold the gun steady nor see my target as anything but a
blur through my tears.

I was in the house when Cole honored my request, my mother
and I holding each other, her seeking the forgiveness I already had
given and me seeking solace. I'm not sure if I cried for two days
or four or six. You never really stop crying over the loss of a loved
one. Nor do you stop loving. Love is kind of like the sun. It can be
warm and gentle, nourishing every part of you, but sometimes
it shines harsh and hard. And it burns. On a ranch, where you
live in the palm of Nature, you learn to accept what that hand
holds—hardships, heartbreaks, adventures, joys, and love.

CHAPTER FOURTEEN

Fame Finds Us

I was walking from the Suburban to the doublewide, my arms full of grocery bags. The wild turkeys marched past me, headed toward the ranch road as if setting out on a summer vacation. One of these days I'd follow them, maybe I'd learn something. Right now I needed to answer the phone ringing inside.

"Hello," I said. The screen door slammed right as the person said his name. "Sorry, didn't hear you."

"This is Kevin Costner calling." There was a pause. "Are you the person to speak to about the wild horse sanctuary?"

"Yes, I am. I'm Alan Day."

"If you have a moment, Mr. Day, I'd like to talk to you about your sanctuary. I'm working on a project involving a lot of horses and you might be of help."

I didn't know anyone named Kevin Costner but said fine, I'd be happy to listen. He proceeded to explain that he was an actor and was directing a movie set in South Dakota. It had to do with Indians and would be filmed on the prairie. He asked a ream of questions about the location of the ranch and its layout, then peppered me with questions about the horses.

"Can you control your horses enough to be able to film them?" he asked.

"You betcha," I said and babbled about how we had trained the horses and could move them in one herd from pasture to pasture.

"They're most cooperative," I said, ever the proud parent. We had not experienced any more wrecks or mishaps since moving day in May.

Costner said, "Several of the scenes involve an Indian camp and a river and a large group of horses that will be used as the remuda."

"Well, we have the Little White River that runs through five miles of the ranch and yes, we can control the horses so they could be filmed as the Indians' ponies," I said.

"I would like to send you a copy of my script and have you read it to see if you can envision the movie being shot on your ranch."

I agreed and we hung up. I walked back outside. The turkeys were fat-rumped specks waddling up the last hill of the road before it turned out of sight. A funny feeling settled over me. That had been a strange conversation. I never went to movies. What if this guy wasn't an actor? What if I was being flimflammed by a hustler? I went back inside and called my buddy Mike Berry in Tucson, the biggest movie buff I knew.

"You ever heard of an actor by the name of Kevin Coogan?" I asked him.

"Kevin Coogan? No, never heard of him."

"Well, some guy named Kevin Coogan just called me and insinuated he's some big movie star and is looking to shoot a film up here on the ranch. I'm wondering if he's for real or giving me a line."

"Kevin Coogan, huh? You sure that's his name?"

"Well, yeah. I'm pretty sure," I said, not feeling so sure. Names and I have never gotten along well. I heard a creak like a chair leaning back and then a hollow slap, like a hand hitting something.

"You wouldn't by chance mean Kevin Costner?"

"Uh, yeah. I might mean Kevin Costner." So I misplaced a few letters. Mike assured me he was the real deal and advised me to rent *Field of Dreams* and *Silverado*. I told him I'd have to get a VCR first.

A few days later, FedEx delivered a box to the ranch. I settled in at my desk, took my pocketknife, slit the end of the box, and slid out a slim black binder filled with a little over a hundred pages of paper. I flipped it open to the first page. *Dances with Wolves*, written by Michael Blake. Every free moment that weekend, I picked up the screenplay. By Sunday night I had finished it. Even with its foreign notations and directions, the story gripped me. I never read a script and didn't have anything to compare it to, but I could envision it being shot on Mustang Meadows Ranch, especially the scenes of an Indian camp on the banks of a river with a horse herd nearby. Costner called midweek and I shared my thoughts.

"If you don't mind, I'd like to come see your ranch and the horses," he said.

"Works with me," I said. We picked a day two weeks out and I filed it in my mental calendar.

I landed my 182 Cessna at the Front Range Airport in Denver and went into the pilot's lounge where Costner and I arranged to meet. He was bringing his producer, Jim Wilson, with him. About ten people were scattered at tables. Two guys in jeans and cowboy boots sat at one. They were about the same age, both with sandy brown hair and athletic. I wasn't sure who was Costner and who was Wilson, so I introduced myself.

Ten minutes later, we boarded the plane; Kevin sat next to me and Jim took the backseat. Kevin mentioned that he had never flown in such a small plane. We taxied out to the run-up area. I picked up my well-used checklist from the dash. I had it memorized but didn't want to appear too nonchalant about piloting, so I went down the list with my finger, checked the steering wheel for free action, cycled the prop, checked oil pressure, checked the mags. Kevin leaned around the seat and said to Jim, "This guy has to read the instruction manual before taking off." Great, I had a comedian and actor on board.

During the seventy-five-minute flight, Kevin told me more about his vision for the movie. It would be his first effort directing. He felt fully confident that he could do it, but Hollywood questioned his ability and refused to put up the money. Eventually he found funds from an investor in Italy. I well knew the language of nay-sayers. It has a limited vocabulary of words like "never," "can't," and "crazy," phrases like "no way," "what's he thinking," and the ultimate wet blanket, "it's impossible." If I had taken the cynics' advice to heart, I might own a ranch in South Dakota, but the only horses on it would be a half-dozen saddle horses. Paddling upstream seemed to be my role in life and Kevin seemed to be sharing the same canoe.

We landed in Valentine and hopped in the Suburban. An hour later, I turned the truck off the state road, driving under the sign, Mustang Meadows Ranch, and past the gnarled post. The sun sat like a ripe peach over the horizon and the hills glowed yellow, as if showing off for Hollywood. "This is how I envisioned it," Kevin said. "This light is perfect."

We turned the corner of the road, drove past the Pitkins' house, and parked. "Guys, we'll have to wait to see the horses and the ranch until tomorrow. How about if I grill some steaks and we have a little dinner?"

"Suits us just fine," said Kevin. They grabbed their duffel bags and I showed them where they would be staying in the doublewide.

We ate steaks and made a dent in a fifth of scotch. Kevin shared his background and his struggle getting into the movie business. He had an easygoing, affable manner about him.

The next morning, before going out to see the ranch and the horses, we stopped by John's house for a cup of coffee. I gave a heads-up hello knock like I always did and let myself in. John was sitting at the table with Jordan and Debbie was scrambling eggs.

"Morning," I said. "Hope you don't mind if I brought a few friends for you to meet." Kevin and Jim followed me into the kitchen and I introduced everyone. To me it was like any other day on the ranch: assess the task in front of you and get it done.

Today's task was to help another man do the best job he could. Debbie sputtered a hello, then froze. John kept looking at her to see if she was going to pass out or stay upright. Later she would tell how she entertained superstar Kevin Costner in her kitchen.

The day was perfect. A brisk breeze, but not enough to dislodge a hat. The greens of early summer. A warm sun. Kevin wanted to know what part of the ranch I owned. How far was it to hotels and restaurants? Where was the Little White River?

"It's just over the next hill," I said.

"Good, then let's park here. I want to see the view as we crest the hill on foot." He explained this was the scene the cameras would reveal. At the top of the hill, we stopped. He framed his hands into a lens and put it up to his eye. "Perfect," I thought I heard him whisper. We spent the rest of the morning in the area. Would he have to get permission to film from anyone but me? No, I owned the property. Could he build a camp here? Yes, no problem. How wide was the river? Do you think these trees work in the background? He was gathering information and making serious decisions. I knew the drill.

The ranch seemed to be calling to him. The location, however, did not. Most of the filming is done in the early morning and late afternoon, when the light is best. Having a crew two hours from the shoot would require everyone to get up at about 3:00 a.m. to start doing makeup, load up, eat breakfast, and then make the trek. That's even early for a cowboy.

It was midafternoon when we drove over to Cemetery pasture, named for the Indian burial mounds on it. I pulled the Suburban up to the crest of a hill. Down below fifteen hundred mustangs grazed. They had become accustomed to the Suburban by now and didn't pay us much attention. A pheasant cock was far less amused by our presence. The bird started running around one of the mounds, squawking. It, in turn, must have amused Kevin, because he got out of the car and started chasing it and doing the funky chicken dance. Maybe he had concentrated so hard by the Little White that he needed an outlet. Jim and I sat in the truck while he squawked and ran. The wind was blowing in the direction of the horses and carried the bird's and Costner's cacophony right into the sensitive ears of the mustangs.

A few horses started pawing the ground. They began to vibrate like a hive of irritated bees, their heads now alert, their tails swishing. Kevin and the pheasant kept up their ritualistic dance. A few of the horses started to run, a signal to the others to pay attention and get moving. Within a minute, the herd was stampeding. Jim and I got out of the truck to watch.

"Costner, look what you've done," yelled Jim. Kevin stopped and looked.

"Oh man," he said. "What happened to them?"

They made a circle of the entire pasture and slowed down once they didn't hear any more grating noise. I wished I had a camera to reveal the scene.

The next day I flew Kevin and Jim up to Pierre to meet with a fellow who owned a herd of buffalo. By then, Kevin knew he loved the land, the river, the horses, but he was discouraged about the logistics. He said that he would let me know if they would be using the ranch. He was a man with a job to do and was taking that job seriously and throwing himself into it. If my ranch fit into that job, then so be it; if not, that was okay too. He said he would love to come back and do some horseback riding and hunting on the ranch. I told him the door was always open.

A few weeks later, Kevin called. He had found a site about fifteen miles outside of Rapid City, South Dakota. It would be better for the crew, but he appreciated being able to see Mustang Meadows Ranch. Sure was a gorgeous place. I wished him luck on his project.

In the end I was glad that the movie wasn't shot on the ranch. A lot of wheels and feet would have trampled the sandy soil in a concentrated area. Surely the grass would have been damaged and who knows what else. I had been concerned about that but reasoned the land would recover post-filming. As it turned out, the movie's incredible popularity resulted in curious people visiting the site where it had been shot. They came at all hours of the day and on all days. With this continuous traffic, the fragile vegetation couldn't recover and blowouts formed, giant potholes caused by high winds. I was glad to enjoy the movie and its scenes of beautiful rolling prairie and not have my ranch damaged. Besides, a few months later, in the fall of 1990, the ranch did end up being filmed for a national audience.

I knew Dayton had been talking to the producers of *20/20*, pitching a segment on the sanctuary. It didn't much interest me, but Dayton was all for public relations. He paid for a chunk of his ranch operations by charging admission for tours and staging fundraising events. The producers bit. They decided to film footage on Dayton's ranch but also wanted to film the larger herd on Mustang Meadows Ranch. The BLM gave their approval in a heartbeat. Positive national publicity about the wild horses rarely came their way.

At first I didn't share the BLM's exuberance, mostly because we were in the middle of one of the driest summers the Midwest had experienced in some years. Even small puffs of wind sent dust skimming over the ground. The filming would require us to move the horses from place to place. Six thousand hooves running across and disturbing dry pastures wasn't exactly part of my land management plan. But as the day for filming approached, an enthusiasm for sharing what we had created and now managed began to grow. Maybe some good would come of it. I probably should have worried that national exposure would encourage competition, but we had such a strong relationship with the BLM, who could possibly compete with us?

The director and film crew must have placed a special order for the day. The morning air felt cool and fresh and the sky's palette was a bright summer blue that heightened the greens and grays of the prairie grass. The rolling hills gave little indication that rain had been scarce. The grass rippled. A sense of pride at what we had accomplished with the sanctuary filled me.

John and I thought it wise to check on the horses before the film crew arrived. We didn't want to be surprised by a sick or crippled horse that might limp in front of the camera and tarnish the glow of all the good things we were doing for the horses. After coffee, we drove out to the pasture adjacent to the corrals to check on the herd. All seemed fine and fit, except that twenty or more head had gotten out of their assigned pasture and stood grazing on the adjacent meadow. How they got out was a mystery, because they probably wouldn't all jump the fence. Was it our phantom?

We had been experiencing a phenomenon that we named "the phantom gate opener." Up to this point, it had always occurred in the north part of the ranch. About once a week, during the night, someone would drive across those north pastures and leave every gate open in his wake. We checked on the horses each day and would find a group that had meandered through the gates. This required us to gather them and return them to their proper pasture and make sure the gates were securely closed. An annoying occurrence that never stopped. The phantom gate opener would strike once every week or two. We never did catch him. The horses learned his game, too. The ones that had gone through knew they were in the wrong place and as soon as they saw us would head straight back through the gate to the right pasture with guilty looks on their faces.

John and I returned to the barn, got on our ATVs, and headed back out to the meadow. We opened the gate and zipped out to fetch the wanderers. They saw us coming. Heads raised and tails swished, but there was no nervous pawing of the ground or gathering. They were asking us in their language what we wanted.

We drove in a wide circle around them, indicating that we wanted them to return to their assigned pasture. They understood. The leader started off toward the gate and pulled the rest of the group in an easy gallop. The gate was about a mile away, and John rode out in front, leading them. I followed behind.

For a moment, I forgot about 20/20 and the filming, forgot about everything I needed to do. As often happened, the beauty of the creatures in front of me pushed out all other thoughts. The elegance of their form and the ease they displayed in running mesmerized me. These weren't groomed-to-the-hilt racehorses with shiny coats. Nobody wanted these horses but me, the cowboys, and this section of the South Dakota Sand Hills. The horses ran with the grasses and the sky, the lines of separation evaporated. The sky, the sun, clouds, horses, grass, hills, horizon. All were one. I cut the motor and listened to the muffled thudding of hooves that made the ground sound hollow and the swish of legs against the grass. Their tails and manes streamed in the air. For a moment, all was right with the world. I restarted the ATV and gunned it to catch up.

The next thing I knew, I was sprawled on the ground, on my stomach, my head turned to one side. I had the sensation of coming out of an afternoon nap where you sleep so hard you can't remember what day it is or where you are. I thought it odd that a piece of metal lay near my outstretched arm. I moved to grab it. Sharp pains jolted me into awareness. That's when I saw the ATV turned on its side. The handlebars were bent down indicating that it had rolled over. The sound of a motor grew louder. I tried to lift my head up, but a jackknife of pain kept it down. The motor roared next to me, then stopped.

John yelled, "Al, are you okay?"

I tried to push up off the ground, a fruitless effort. All I could do was groan. John's boots and jeans appeared.

"Roll me on my side," I said.

"Let's not rush this. Let's make sure everything's intact."

I gingerly moved muscles and limbs. Neither of us thought my neck or back were injured, but the condition of my left shoulder, sides, hips, and right ankle were a far different state of affairs. The pain shot right into my gut. I concentrated on not throwing up. John tried to lift me into a standing posture, but I slumped to the ground. I needed to get to a hospital, but it would be an hour before an ambulance could arrive.

"Go get the Suburban and Debbie," I said. It hurt to talk. "If you can get me in there, she can take me to the hospital. Put some padding in it and a pillow."

His mind must have gone through the same scenario. "Yep, the ranch ambulance. I'm on it."

He fetched my hat from the grass ten yards away and helped settle me against the wheel of the ATV. For the time being, the grass was a soft mattress.

"Promise I won't go anywhere," I said. He looked like he didn't want to leave but hopped on the ATV and drove off. The drone of the motor dwindled. I concentrated on breathing and not moving for what seemed like an hour. I tried to figure out what might have caused the wreck, but my last memory was of the horses galloping ahead. The breeze pressed against the cold sweat covering me. At last, I heard the grumble of the Suburban. John backed it up close to my slumped body. Debbie jumped out and came over, concern spread across her face. Somehow, the three of us managed to get me up and into the makeshift ambulance.

"John, look around. See if you can find what I hit." He never did find any object, hole, or camouflaged outcropping.

I lay on the blankets in the back and marveled at how uneven the ground really was. The road was even worse. And here I thought we had smoothed it out.

We rolled through a pothole that must have been a mile deep. "Deb, I'm not dying back here. You don't have to race to the hospital," I said. "Any more bumps like that last one and you'll have to find me a stick to bite." I'd bite it in half. I focused on inhaling and exhaling, which wasn't the easiest task. Highway 20 felt like a paradise of freshly asphalted roadway. It afforded the opportunity for a few thoughts to seep in.

What was happening at the ranch? How long would it take the production crews to set up? Where would they film? I was pretty certain the horses would perform well. I hadn't wanted the crew to come, but now I was bummed at missing the event. John was more than capable of handling the horses and people. But still. In between the throbs of pain, frustration pulsed at having had the wreck and now lying immobile in the back of the Suburban. By the time we finally pulled into the emergency entrance at Cherry County Hospital in Valentine, Nebraska, I was one ornery, beat-up mess.

The doctor on duty immediately ordered X-rays and said I would be spending the night, so I sent Debbie home. By midafternoon, the diagnosis came in: a separated shoulder, a broken ankle, cracked ribs, and a bruised hip. Thank God I had rolled on sandy soil and not concrete. I was wheeled into a room and moved onto a bed. All I wanted to do was lie still. Nurses and doctors kept looking in on me. Just as I was dozing, a nurse said my blood pressure was too low. Five minutes later a doctor arrived.

"We think maybe you're bleeding internally," he said, "but we don't have a way to test that. The best thing to do is load you on an airplane and send you up to the Mayo Clinic in Rochester, Minnesota."

I said, "No, I think I'll just stay here."

"We're just a little country hospital. This isn't the place for you."

"Well, I feel like I've already gone five hundred miles today. I'm used up. I hurt in places that I didn't know could hurt. I'm tired. I need a nice, warm, soft place to rest."

"But you're not understanding. We think this is serious. We're recommending airlifting you."

"Yeah, I understand. But my answer is no. I'm not going there."

The doctor and nurse looked totally frustrated. "What would you want us to do if we didn't have enough blood to sustain you and here you are in Valentine and not in Rochester?"

"I do understand what you're saying to me. My answer is you'll either fix me up or I'll die. And I'm okay with either."

They left in a huff. I could hear them in the hall discussing my possible demise. Someone said, "Let's send for Dr. Trimble because this idiot cowboy doesn't get it. Maybe he can talk some sense into him."

In a little bit here came Dr. Cleve Trimble. He looked at my eyes and demeanor and color and talked to me enough to know I wasn't out of my head. For the next two hours, we chatted about all kinds of things, except for the wreck—our lives, our goals, and the tracks that took both of us to this very spot. We formed a lasting friendship. By the time he left, I just wanted to sleep and gather strength. Sometime during the night a nurse woke me to take my blood pressure. It had rebounded and was strong.

The next morning, I announced that Debbie would get me. Dr. Trimble said that he wanted to keep me another day.

"I can stay quiet at the ranch just as well as here," I said.

"Well if you're going to be that hardheaded, you have to get out to the front door without assistance or a wheelchair."

A nurse brought in a set of crutches, and I proceeded to take a few steps. My body let me have it, but I managed to crutch my way out to the front door. It took forty minutes. Debbie and the Suburban were waiting with the passenger door opened. As I climbed in every joint and muscle screamed, then subsided into a low roar.

Debbie pulled away from the entrance. "Is there anything I can get you?"

I knew exactly what I needed. Dairy Queen. I placed my order and Debbie came back with vanilla-chocolate twist soft serve ice cream in a cone. Maybe I had died, because it sure did taste like heaven.

Later John came over to the doublewide to fill me in on the day's details. The horses responded just as we had trained them to do. At the director's request, John had moved them—all fifteen hundred—to different pastures. The horses looked great, Dayton presented himself nicely on the program, and everyone was happy—everyone but me, lying grumpy and sore in a hospital bed. After hours of filming, John advised the director that the horses were telling him they were tired of being hassled. The director insisted on one last shot of the herd galloping over the top of a hill toward the cameraman filming at the bottom. John reluctantly agreed but warned, "Tell your cameraman to get his footage on the first try, because there won't be another opportunity."

He waited until the cameraman was in position at the foot of the hill. "You better be ready," John advised him. "When they come over the hill, they'll be going so fast they'll be past you before you know it." The cameraman signaled that he was ready. I can only imagine what he felt when he heard the hooves of more than a thousand horses thundering and felt the earth vibrating. They came over the hill right at him, then split around him on both sides; he was so traumatized that he forgot to push the start button on the camera. Rumor had it from those who were there that he appeared to wet his pants as the horses swept by.

All in all, the 20/20 folks were quite pleased with the program. In fact, it earned the show an Emmy for nature photography. We always wondered how much better it might have been if the cameraman had gotten that last shot. The BLM people were pleased, too, as the show put the wild horses and our management of them in a kind light. Our friends who saw the 20/20 program asked where I was. I don't imagine the program would have changed much if I had been there.

All my injuries healed in time except for my shoulder, which I never bothered to have surgery on. Now, when the weather turns cold, it still reminds me of the ATV ride that morning in South Dakota. The lump formed by the displaced bone looks odd, but I'm not fixin' to enter any beauty pageants, at least not in the near future. Once again, life taught me that mishaps can occur at the most unexpected of times.

The sun peeked over the edge of Lazy B's rolling eastern hills. Aunt Jemima and I had already ridden four miles from Big Tank, where we were rounding up that day. It was a large area to cover, about twelve square miles. I had a crew of eight, but they were out of sight, working their designated areas.

We had gotten out of bed at 3:30 a.m., downed a breakfast of steak, eggs, and black coffee, and bounced in the pickup the five miles to Big Tank, where the roundup would start. The previous night we had left our horses there with extra feed in the corral. Each cowboy caught his horse and saddled up. It was Aunt Jemima's turn to be ridden and she let me know by the swing of her head and stomp of her feet she was up to it. So here we were, Jemima and me and about thirty head of cattle. I couldn't see anyone else. The hands riding on either side of me were about a mile away, hills and canyons separating us. Jemima and I herded the cattle toward Tank 4, a dirt water hole that had been bulldozed out of a rocky canyon years before. From there we would go down toward Big Tank and, on the way, hook up with the other cowboys and the rest of the herd.

The cattle drove easily toward Tank 4. It was about 9:00 a.m. when we arrived. The spring air had shrugged off its cool temperature under the growing heat of the sun. The cattle were thirsty from clomping through dust and stopped to drink from the pond. Jemima and I followed the last cows to the water. The leaders had gotten their fill and were filing out onto the trail. Jemima and I walked around the tank to gather the remaining cattle and have them follow their mates. All of sudden Jemima stopped and grunted. Her weight shifted. She looked back at me, her eyes pleading for help. Nothing in front of us looked alarming or out of the ordinary. Perplexed, I looked back. Her right hind leg was raised.

"What's going on, Jemima?" I said. I patted her hip, but she remained rooted in place. I dismounted to have a look. A stick dangled from the inside of her right thigh. It was a curved creosote stick about a foot long with a circumference about as large as my thumb. She must have stepped on one end of the stick and the other end went flying into her. I gently pulled on it, but there was no give. It must have wedged in her muscle, which meant it had penetrated deeply. No wonder she stopped. She wouldn't be able to take another step with that stick in her leg. It needed to come out right here, right now.

"Hang tight, Jemima. This may hurt."

With one quick motion, I yanked out the stick. She jumped and tried to move away but couldn't put weight on her right leg. Blood gushed. Within seconds it began to rhythmically pump, spilling in a dark-red pool on the dirt. I pushed my thumb against the puncture wound. The blood ran down my arm and dripped off my elbow. It ran down Jemima's leg. The puddle on the ground formed a dark tributary that flowed toward my boot. Jemima's thigh quivered. The pain had to be severe. The blood ran fast. I wondered how long it takes for a horse to bleed to death.

I spoke to calm us both down. "Jemima, wow. This is really something. But you're holding steady. I need you to keep doing that while I get something to stop this bleeding." With my free hand, I dug in the rear pocket of my Levis for my handkerchief. From the front pocket, I retrieved my pocketknife. Keeping my thumb pressed against the wound, I managed to cut a piece of fabric and wad it into a ball. I stuffed it into the bleeding hole. Almost immediately, it became soaked, but the blood went from pumping to dribbling down her leg in rivulets. The ground under her now was stained. I had so much blood on my shirt, chaps and the leg of one jean I could have been mistaken for the injured.

Jemima knew I was trying to help. She hadn't kicked or tried to move my hands away. We were a team and we were going to get through this fix.

"There aren't any roads up here, Jemima, and even if there were, we don't have a trailer to haul you home." I wiped my hands as best I could on my shirt, then rubbed reassuringly on her thigh and flank. "I think the bleeding is starting to slow. We'll give it another ten minutes, but then we're going to have to move and figure out how to get down to Big Tank."

She turned her head slightly and flipped one ear forward. I stayed on the ground and kept my eye on the seeping wound. When I couldn't detect flowing blood, I stood up. The cattle had long since gone, but they were the least of my worries. They had been through gentling school and wouldn't try to escape. Right now, I needed Jemima to put down her leg and take a step.

"Okay, we're gonna give this a try. I'm going to lead you down the path. We'll take it slow." I took the bridle reins and moved in front of her. She stood stock still. "Come on, Jemima," I said, giving the reins a tug. She didn't offer to follow and her leg remained in the air. The pain must have been too great. What could I do? This was one serious mess.

"Jemima, damnit, you have to lead. We have to work together. What's it going to take?" We stood there looking at each other.

If she wouldn't lead, I'd have to drive her. I wrapped the reins around the saddle horn. If she had ever desired freedom, she was probably miffed it came now. I found a stick a few yards away, got behind her and tapped her with it. She put her leg down and hobbled a few steps. It was painful to watch; she could bear only a little of her weight on the right leg. We started our slow journey, Jemima with her heavy limp and me in my heavy chaps and heeled boots. After a hundred yards, I yelled to her. "Whoa,

Jemima, whoa." She heard the tone of my voice and stopped. I caught up and bent down to examine the wound. There was no fresh blood on her leg. The plug was holding.

"We're doing okay here," I said, rubbing and loving on her. "We're on our way to Big Tank. Sooner or later the other cowboys will see we're behind and they'll come back and help us. But for now we have to keep making our way down the trail."

We started out again. My spur rowels clanked on the stones. I've always thought cowboys walking with all their paraphernalia look out of place. I'm sure the hawks soaring overhead and the chipmunks darting between their desert holes thought so too. In another hundred yards, I called, "Whoa, Jemima, whoa." I caught up with her, checked on her wound, and gave her another pep talk. And so we haltingly made our way downhill along the dirt cobbled with lava rock. Had there been shade, it would have been as tempting as ice cream, but there was only the beating sun.

Forty-five minutes later we caught up with the cows. They had followed the trail toward Big Tank but with no one pushing them, they had stopped and were dillydallying and eating grass. Before I realized what was happening, Jemima walked off the path, got around a cow, and drove her back to the trail. I was astounded. I had seen cow dogs go after cattle and bring them back, but never a horse. Horses don't work cattle without a rider. But here was Jemima, still nursing a wound, stiff with pain, and off she went without me saying one word. It was just like Jemima to stay engaged in the activity at hand. If I was out working cattle, she wanted to work cattle and be part of the process. Well, she was being part of the process right now, just like she would have been if I had been on her. We remained a team.

As we got closer to Big Tank, we had less area to cover, so the distance between us and the other cowboys narrowed. They could see Jemima walking and me walking, each working our side. One of the hands came riding up.

"Well, I see your horse is more cowboy than you today," he said, and turned to spit. "You're not cowboy enough to ride her, but she's cowboy enough to keep driving the cattle." He suppressed a grin. I showed him the wound. "I'll be damned," he said. "I never saw a horse work cattle without a rider."

By now the limp was slight. I got on her to see if she could carry my weight. Yes, she could. The team came in as one.

I put her in the small corral we had, got in the pickup, and drove back to headquarters to get a trailer. After I hauled her home, I doctored her with antibiotics. Despite the dust and dirty handkerchief, the wound never became infected. It healed so rapidly, in fact, that two weeks later, Jemima and I were out riding again.

Of course that day bonded Aunt Jemima and me even closer. I knew she had a big heart, but its depth amazed me. She had the stuff you need out on the range when you're miles from nowhere and no one—true grit and loyalty. From that day on, whenever I said, "Whoa, Jemima," she stopped. Whether she was in the pasture or corral, eating or working, she'd stop and wait for me. I'd come up to her and rub her head, her neck, and speak softly and sweetly to her. Because that's what you do when you have a partner. You give them as much love as they give you.

CHAPTER FIFTEEN

On Thin Ice

We had to get there. Even on gusty mornings when tiny, sharp snowflakes stung our eyes and cheeks and the cold snaked through our jeans and gloves. That's when we ditched the spurred leather boots for lined waffle stompers with thick rubber soles. Better traction on iced mud and drifting snow. We pulled our wool caps down as far as they went, slid our hands in gloves, and headed toward the barn. Some days the gray sky hung so low I was tempted to prop it up with tent poles. Other times it fell, in millions of crystal pieces that blanketed the ground white. Regardless, the cowboys and I had to get out there. We had to feed the horses and cattle.

At least we had it easier than our midwestern forefathers. They didn't have a heated tractor cab with windshield wipers. Or a bale wagon that loaded five bales at a time, each weighing fifteen hundred pounds, then ground them up and spread them in a long pyramid across the pastures. We needed twenty-five to thirty pounds of hay per mustang, which equated to fourteen bales of hay per day. If our machinery broke down, as it was prone to do, we radioed back to headquarters and had someone haul out a new part or the backup tractor and feeder kept on the premises for emergencies. Before a blizzard hit, we moved the livestock closer to headquarters, behind the tree claims. Even then, a whiteout might obscure the horses or stacks of hay. We drove slowly. Tried not to run over a horse or fence. Felt our way over the ground.

Weekday. Weekend. Holiday.

Sun. Rain. Hail. Wind. Lightning. Snow. Ice.

Feeding the horses was as much a responsibility as feeding our families. Even without the government contracts entrusting the horses to our care, we would have done it. For the love of horses, we did it.

I checked the clock before answering the phone. Six a.m. Late for a cowboy, but not for a cowboy the morning after popping corks off champagne bottles to ring in the New Year.

"Hullo."

"Al, it's John. Sorry to wake you so early on New Year's Day, but at the moment we've got a rather unhappy scene up here." His voice held an uncharacteristic tension.

"What's going on, John?"

"I don't know if you saw a weather report recently, but yesterday it got pretty warm. During the afternoon some horses broke through the ice on the pond over in the leased meadow. About fourteen drowned. I just can't believe it. The ice still looks to be a foot thick. The warmth must have weakened it and with the weight of several hundred crossing over, well . . . damn. Somehow the sheriff and county attorney got wind of it and they came knocking at the door this morning before we had the coffee going. The county attorney was most unfriendly."

Whoa. Now, that's like getting a bucket of ice water dumped over your head. In an instant, it dissolved the fog hovering around my brain but took my breath away and sent chills down my spine.

"Well, why would the sheriff and county attorney be there? What reason would they have to be involved?"

"The county attorney is talking cruelty to animals, possibly starvation." Before I could wrap my head around that one, John continued. "The local TV station in Sioux Falls picked up on the news. A reporter has been wandering around out front, and a helicopter's been flying overhead pretty low for the past hour, scaring the shit out of the horses. Marty said they're running around like nervous wrecks."

Holy Moses. I had fallen asleep on a smooth-running train that derailed during the night and now lay in a crumpled mess. But one thing I knew. When an emergency hits, you get your ass in gear. Fast. Even if it means leaving your home on a holiday.

"I'm coming up there, John. Tell the sheriff and county attorney I'll be available to talk to them tomorrow. Or tonight if need be."

I could almost feel John relax over the phone. "Okay, I'll tell them," he said. "This isn't the first time animals have fallen through the ice and died. The Randall Ranch lost a thousand head of steers some years back. But I've never seen a reaction like this."

"We'll sort it out when I get there," I said. "Right now I need to check the weather, make a flight plan, and top off the fuel tank. I'll be wheels up within the hour."

I hung up and flopped back on my pillow. Sue burrowed next to me.

"Doesn't sound good," she said. I looked at the ceiling, so white and clean, like fresh snow. A sliver of hopeful sunshine ran its length. Who would have thought of horses falling through melting ice? This wasn't in the handbook of my upbringing.

"I'll make a burrito and fill a thermos of coffee. You can take them on the plane," Sue said.

I rolled over and hugged her. Sustenance before the storm.

Flying twenty thousand feet above the problems of the world for four hours afforded me time to think. The problem was I didn't know what to think. Had I been careless? Or was this an unavoidable act of nature? We always watched the weather reports for winter storms, but in this case we should have been watching for a warming trend. If the possibility of this tragedy wasn't on my radar screen, was I liable for it? And what exactly did "liable" mean?

The plane's wheels touched down on the dry runway. The midafternoon sun splayed its golden rays between islands of gray clouds. The icy air gave no indication that its warmer cousin had been in town. By now the pond probably had refrozen. Knowing that I would soon see the herd and the victims and be able to assess the situation soothed my anxiety.

An hour later, John and I powwowed in his kitchen over hot coffee.

"First, a bit of bad news," said John.

"Like there hasn't been enough already?"

He smiled in a weary sort of way. "One of the mares tried to jump the fence when that chopper was buzzing around, but she didn't quite clear it. Marty and I found her caught in the barbed wire. She was already dead."

Early on, we had noticed the horses react to the sound of a helicopter. If they heard even a distant thump, thump, thump, they would gather and go to running. I could just see it. The news helicopter circling, low and buzzing, just like when the same angry bird captured the horses in the wild. Surely they panicked and ran blindly in all directions, haunted by this past life nightmare. The pilot probably had no clue about the fear he incited. All he saw below was a bunch of wild, crazed, presumably untrained horses. Here I was trying to protect the horses and keep them as stress free as possible. If there was cruelty to animals, it was that fucking helicopter. What was that county attorney thinking, going to the media before we had a chance to talk? Especially since the drowning didn't seem to be an unprecedented event.

"Tell me about what happened at the Randall Ranch," I said. The details might be fodder for tomorrow's meeting.

John relayed the sad story. Eight years ago, in the middle of January, a big norther blew in and whipped its white fury on the land for three days. The Randall steers were in a pasture north of a large lake, but the blizzard dropped so much snow it covered all the fences. The cattle drifted southeast, away from the storm, right over those concealed posts and barbed wire. The entire herd tramped out onto the lake. One thousand cattle weighing in at six hundred pounds each. The ice gave way and the cattle crashed through into the frigid water and drowned. No one charged the owner with wrongdoing for the simple reason he had done nothing wrong. He ultimately paid for the accident with bankruptcy. Lost his ranch and ended up moving to a different state.

"It happens," said John. "That's the worst case I know of. And no one said anything beyond 'I'm sorry for your loss.'"

My heart went out to this stranger, this fellow rancher who succumbed to what can be a blessing or a curse: the weather. Sometimes the clouds roll in on cue and other times they leave you high and dry. I looked out the window. The sun was calling it a day. I'd have to postpone a visit to the pond until tomorrow, though first on the agenda would be a meeting with the county attorney.

I walked over to the kitchen phone and dialed the number on the card the county attorney had given John. He was unavailable, so I left a message saying we would be there by nine o'clock the next morning.

Debbie came in to start dinner, with Megan skipping behind her. "Megan, set a place for Alan."

Megan opened a cabinet and took out placemats. "You sit here tonight," she said, laying one in front of me, "and I'll sit here." She laid another placemat next to mine.

"I wouldn't want to sit by anyone else but my girl," I said. It was a comfort at a time like this to be surrounded by people who cared.

John and I retired to the family room to watch the news. The county attorney had been effective in his media campaign. The local CBS station reported that more than a dozen wild horses had drowned in a pond outside of Winner, South Dakota. Alan Day, owner of Mustang Meadows Ranch, was being investigated for animal abuse, the newscaster said over a clip of the horses filmed from the helicopter. The mustangs ran in all directions, manes and tails flying, as frantic as I had imagined. Distraught from abuse, a viewer might conclude. So much for my mitigating any further damage to the situation; the intensity had just quadrupled. The local news ended and the national news began.

Halfway through the broadcast, Debbie called us to dinner. John was about to turn off the TV when the newscaster said, "And now from South Dakota, a tragedy on a government-sponsored wild horse sanctuary." Good grief. A wire service must have picked up the story. Millions of eyes around the country saw the same dramatic images of panicked horses. I almost could hear the collective groan from the BLM executives watching the news from their homes. It echoed mine. Definitely not the publicity I had described to the BLM back in DC.

John flipped off the TV. The New Year was less than forty-eight hours old and already it had snowballed into an avalanche.

I have participated in negotiations with tension levels ranging from one to ten. Even those strung taut with anger and anxiety managed to start with a protocol of pleasantries. A hello and shaking of hands, an offer of coffee and a chair. Except for an unemotional handshake, the pleasantries at the county attorney's office in Winner were frigid. Even my "How you doin'?" didn't elicit a response from the stern-looking man fortressed behind his desk. John and I pulled up chairs and sat down. I sensed it was up to us to get the conversation rolling.

"I received the call about the horses yesterday morning at my Arizona ranch," I said. "Within forty minutes I was in my plane. It took the better part of the day to get here, but here I am, eager to sort out any problems we have." The county attorney's face could have been chiseled in the granite of Mount Rushmore. "But you're going to have to help me, because I'm not sure exactly what those problems are."

Starchy silence filled the room. I forged ahead. "John mentioned that you had been out at the ranch yesterday morning and saw the horses in the pond and made some statements to the press about possible criminal activity. I saw the segment on the news last night. Local and national." This time the man on the other side of the desk nodded. "But I'm having a hard time grasping just what the criminal activity is. How do horses breaking through melting ice translate into a legal or moral or emotional crisis?"

"The newscast was correct. We are proceeding with a criminal investigation."

"I don't understand. What possible criminal activities could there be?"

"Mr. Day, there's no reason for you to be here talking to me. You'll have to wait for the investigation."

"That's fine. I'll wait," I said, my voice filling the room. "But there has to be something you're investigating."

The county attorney huffed like he was dealing with some sort of remedial student. "Our office has cause to believe that the horses under your care are being starved, which would constitute cruelty to animals. We don't know what we're going to uncover here. We are proceeding with an investigation."

If a person can go into shock two days in a row, I did. What did this noodlehead know about our operation? "Those horses are fed and watered each day. We've had them for three years and we've never missed a day feeding them." The man on Planet X sitting on the opposite side of the desk gave me a cool stare. "I'm not sure what your goal is here or why you're even involved," I said.

"This happens at least every five to ten years when we get a sudden thaw," said John. "Livestock fall through the melting ice and drown."

The attorney didn't bite. "If you're abusing them, I intend to put you in jail, Mr. Day." He glared me down like I was a danger to society and we would all be safer if I was off the streets and in prison. He didn't even bother to fake remorse for the death of the animals. "I want to postmortem six horses to determine if they're malnourished."

This guy had his legal pistol cocked and aimed at me. But what the hell was there to find? Only horses with full stomachs, certainly.

"I have no issue with that," I said. "Give me the name of your vet, and we'll get them over as soon as we cut them out. The cold last night froze them and I suspect they're in about two feet of ice."

He reached for a pad of paper and pen.

"How will I know when this investigation is over?" I asked.

"The statute of limitations is seven years. You'll know by then," he said. He scribbled on the paper and pushed it across the desk.

John nodded in recognition of the name. "I know where his office is," he said.

I tapped the paper on the desk. "I still don't understand," I said, truly clueless to what this guy was thinking and planning. "How long is this investigation going to take? Seven years?"

The lifted chin, the cool stare. "We'll come for you with handcuffs if we want to press charges," he said and stood up.

No pleasantries concluded the meeting.

I climbed into the pickup's cab mystified. What was this fellow after?

"You're a big fish around here, Alan," said John when I shared my befuddlement. "If our friendly county attorney lands you in jail, he can slap that on his resume and present it to voters. It's like saying, 'I brought in the bad guy, vote for me.'"

That thought had never even occurred to me. I was just doing my job. But now, as I was doing it, I stood face to face with someone intent on using this tragedy to stoke his career ambitions rather than balancing the scales of justice. Locking me up behind bars was just the fuel to fan his campaign flames. I felt like I was being profiled and convicted before being tried. But what ground did he have for charges?

"John, did you feed those horses every day?

"Hell yes. You know we feed them every day."

"And are you feeding them the full ration of thirty pounds of hay per day?

"Yes, of course. We never miss a day."

"Well goddamn, he's punching at air."

We ate a quick lunch at the house, then loaded the pickup with chainsaws, boards, ropes, chains, and other tools we might need. John drove the big blue Ford tractor with the front-end loader attached, and we convoyed across the frozen prairie. The fresh dusting of snow on the road wouldn't sit still in the wind. We bumped along the icy ground, the wipers smearing tiny flakes across the pickup's windshield. Thankfully the clouds were not predicted to drop much snow. Three gates and thirty minutes later we entered the leased pasture, the scene of the supposed crime.

The pond lay over a few hills and to the left. The dark silhouettes of eight hundred less fourteen horses dotted the meadow. We had not discussed moving the herd. Even with the drowning, no rancher would have moved horses in the middle of winter away from a meadow with blocked-up hay and fresh water.

John and I walked out onto the semiclear ice. Dark, eerie shapes lay under its surface. I could make out blurred manes and tails, legs bent at odd angles, horses layered on top of each other. The side of one horse tilted downward like a submarine going under, its head out of sight. We walked, looking through the ice like you look through a glass-bottom boat. I thought of Candy and the waves from one panicked horse. Imagine thirty, forty, or perhaps, as John suspected and a neighbor reported, several hundred horses fighting for their lives in frigid waters. God, it must have been pure pandemonium for what—five, ten minutes? For a moment I heard the hollow cracking of ice and the panicked snorts, the high-pitched whinnies pleading above the turbulent splash of water. Then stillness. Even with the wind howling its grief, there would have been that stillness. I had experienced that stillness once and would never forget its empty sound.

We unloaded the truck. I fired up a chainsaw and pushed the screaming blade into the ice near the rump of the horse closest to the surface. Cutting around it was easy work. Lifting the animal-embedded ice block proved trickier. First, we had to get a chain around some part of the horse. That meant dunking our arms up to the elbow in the icy water so we could finagle the metal links around a leg, a neck, a hip. The ice had refrozen to two feet thick, but water slopped up and over our boots. Once the chain was secure, we could attach it to the tractor and pull. Sometimes we needed to pry a body part lose from the ice or another horse with a board or set the board at an angle below the horse so we could leverage it onto a clear area. There, we'd chip away ice chunks around the carcass, then drag it to shore. Slipping and sliding and sweating, we improvised and became more efficient as we went. We didn't dismember one horse.

Four hours later, we hauled the last horse ashore. I had accumulated a lifetime quota of this job. Using the tractor's front-end loader, we stacked six horses in the trailer behind the pickup. Enough afternoon remained for John to transport them to the vet. He headed out the back way, not bothering to return to headquarters to change his wet jeans. In the cowboy handbook, personal comfort takes the backseat to getting the job done.

I climbed in the tractor cab and blasted the heat. Maybe someday I'd wise up about buying ranches in this climate.

Debbie, bless her heart, invited me to dinner again. The hearty smell of beef stew and the kids' chatter about their first day back to school seeped like fresh springwater into the part of me that had drained since leaving Arizona. We all gathered to watch the local news. It concluded with a story about Mustang Meadows Ranch. Here we go again, I thought. But the newscaster slid a surprise in front of us. She said the station was retracting its story about the wild horses being mistreated. Upon further investigation, it was determined that the horses received regular feed and water but had accidentally broken through thawing ice. These are the ravishments of winter on the plains, she said, a travesty that couldn't be avoided. She looked appropriately solemn.

What constituted "further investigation" beat me. As far as I knew, in the past twenty-four hours the wind hadn't blown in any reporters, detectives, or strangers to dig up new information. This mystery I welcomed; it didn't threaten handcuffs. Maybe the county attorney had tuned in to the broadcast.

Later that evening in the doublewide, the phone rang. Expecting it to be Sue, I was surprised to hear a neighbor's voice. He extended condolences about the drowning.

"I saw the story on the news, and it irritated me a good piece. I know you boys are out there feeding those horses every day. So I went and called up the station and told them just that. I'm pretty sure there's a few other folks around here did the same thing."

Gotta love neighbors coming to the rescue with a phone call. I didn't need a more temperate climate. This one had more warmth tucked in it than I realized.

The vet completed the autopsies the next afternoon, and John drove back to fetch the carcasses. The vet told John that the report he would turn into the county attorney would say all the horses had hay in their stomachs and a layer of fat over their backs. John unloaded the six next to the other dead horses at the edge of the pond. Now fourteen mangled horses needed to be disposed of. The BLM owned the horses; it was their call what to do with them. I had been keeping the manager of the Sturgis office abreast of events. He knew what kind of program we ran on Mustang Meadows Ranch and, despite the fifteen minutes of sour publicity, offered me the agency's full support. I rang him to share the vet's findings.

"Well, darn, if that isn't finally some good news."

"No kidding," I said. "But now we have to do something with the carcasses. They're lying out there next to the pond."

"What do you suggest we do with them?" he asked.

I had been grappling with this conundrum earlier in the day. The last thing I wanted was for some politically motivated person to send a shutterbug out to sensationalize the utterly gruesome pile of horses in a photo story with my name smeared across the front of it. "I suggest you tell me to bury them and to do it as soon as possible."

He didn't skip a beat. "Alan, you need to bury those horses and do it tomorrow, if not sooner."

I called the county attorney next. "The BLM has instructed me to bury the horses and I wanted to let you know that I'm going to be doing that tomorrow morning."

"That's tampering with evidence, Mr. Day. I could have you arrested for that," he said, still prancing around like a cock sure of winning the fight.

"Well, then you best take it up with the BLM, because they own the horses. Or get yourself a cease and desist order because I've been given orders by my contractor and I aim to follow them."

"We may need to come out and dig them up if we need evidence."

"Then you do that, but right now, I want to get them buried. There's no humane reason to keep them above ground."

I felt like I had called his bluff. I owned the ranch. I signed the BLM contract. And now I was being proactive and calling the shots. Still, I didn't trust the man for a minute. He might just show up.

I knew exactly where to bury the horses—on the land adjacent to the leased pasture where they had drowned, between the first set of hills in a fairly level swale. Other than a concrete foundation, the remnant of a small barn or maybe a cowpoke's home, it was pure prairie. John had moved the horses out there already and offered to help dig the hole, but I didn't want to drag him any further into this mess. The buck stopped with me, and this part was all mine. I suggested he hang around headquarters. If the county attorney showed up, he could give him a lift in the pickup out to the pasture. "Offer him a cup of coffee first," I said.

I hopped on the backhoe and started the trek out to the pasture. There was no heated cab but the bright sun warmed my face. The white hills rolled before me flecked with the tops of dormant grass. When I crested the last hill, I could see the pile of horses below, legs and heads at odd, ugly angles.

It took me a good hour to dig a hole large enough to bury all fourteen. I deposited the horses in the hole and pushed dirt over them, then smoothed it out perfectly flat. But I needed a burial marker. The concrete foundation had been built using two-by-two-foot slabs, and the backhoe scooped them up like a piece of cake. It was just about lunchtime when I set the last concrete slab in place. I took one last look at my handiwork. Yep, it was a proper grave, and this proper grave was one that wouldn't be easy to dig up.

I called the BLM to debrief them. The rep patted my back. He paused for a moment, then said, isn't it something that those horses got all this attention, and the Native American guy who ran out of gas on a county road near Sturgis and froze to death in his car about the same time the horses drowned never received so much as a mention from the media?

I never heard from the county attorney again, nor did any television reporter or animal rights activists wave the cruelty to animals flag in my face. The incident died and was buried in the grave of county lore. Except for a little worm that snuck out seven months later.

On a quiet August evening, humidity hanging heavy on the air, the phone rang. The man on the other end introduced himself as the sheriff in the horse-drowning incident. His term had expired and he decided the time had come to move to a warmer climate. He was considering Arizona. He hoped to supplement his retirement with a job as a night watchman or some sort of security personnel. Did I know anywhere he might apply? I gave him some suggestions and names. He thanked me, then said, "I've been wanting to tell you the rest of story about those horses."

He went on to say that the county attorney had requested a report from him about the drowning. But the county attorney said, "I want to write it and you to sign it." The sheriff said no. "I'll do the investigation and I'll write the report and sign it." His investigation consisted of talking to eight neighbors to determine what kind of ranchers we were. Did we starve our horses? Were they fed and watered every day? Did we ever abuse them in the corrals with whips or out on the pasture? Every single neighbor said no, those boys take pride in treating the horses nicely. They have them on fresh feed. They put up several thousand tons of hay each year and feed it to the horses all winter. He said his investigation convinced him that there was no abuse.

"I told that to the county attorney," he said. "Really pissed him off."

So the attorney's attempt to land a big fish flopped before it hit dry land. Maybe I had dodged a bullet. Maybe the county attorney's case would have sunk before it sailed too far into the court system. At least this time the hand of justice didn't hold any trick cards. As I would learn, that didn't always prove to be true.

PART THREE

CHAPTER SIXTEEN

Horses of Many Colors

I told Russ to top off the motorcycles with gas and then fix the fence in the meadow. I'd do the morning rounds out on the Whitelands pasture. The horses had been grazing there for the past two weeks, and I wanted to examine the grass and also see if the phantom gate opener had been at work again. But first I needed to check on Sally and Blue.

Sally saw me walking toward her corral and met me at the fence. A small sorrel, she plopped her nose on the top bar hoping to be petted. "You are a glutton for loving, aren't you?" I said, brushing her long mane out of her eyes and rubbing on her. She angled her back within my reach. In the adjacent corral, Blue stood patiently awaiting her turn.

The BLM had granted us permission to select a few horses from the herd and try to break them. It took a bit of wheedling. They held firm against my pleas, saying that our guardianship didn't permit us to do that. Every time we went out with the herd, two horses stepped out front to greet us.

"Why not bring those two in and see what happens?" I argued. "I want to get in their minds. See what they like and don't like. Maybe we'll learn something."

The BLM finally conceded and said we could break those two if we later turned them back into the herd. John and I gathered them, the mare that Megan named Sally and a blue roan filly we simply called Blue.

I gave Sally a pat on the rump and walked over to do due diligence with Blue. She pushed her nose into my palm. The horses had been in the corrals for a week now. I wasn't sure how either would respond to being brought in, but they acted like they had submitted a transfer request and were pleased as punch to have it honored. They willingly accepted a halter and lead rope, even more so than many domestic horses, and within a day, could be led into the barn, where they learned to eat grain out of a manger. I was tickled they were mirroring the respect and care we had shown them since their arrival at the ranch.

"I'll get back to you later, girl." Blue bobbed her head against my arm as if she didn't want me to leave. "I'll introduce you to Alan Jr. He's coming up later today for a week." I had told Al about Sally and Blue and he offered to break them during his visit. Blue pawed an acknowledging hoof and meandered off toward some hay strewn on the ground. I went to find a motorcycle.

The June morning offered up the scent of healthy plants and a hint of impending summer humidity. I chugged through the pastures at the leisurely pace permissible on a Saturday. I turned the dirt bike south and proceeded up a hill thinking the herd might be on the other side. The horses liked to hang out where the sun spent the afternoons. Sure enough, there they were. I braked to a stop and put a foot down. My eye had developed the habit of settling on horses I had come to know. Happy always landed on my radar screen first. With his bright black-and-white splotches, he stood out, handsome and stately, regardless of where he grazed, which tended to be at the outskirts of the herd. Almost every visitor at the ranch commented on him. Even the BLM reps who visited quarterly knew him. "Happy's looking good," they would say. Did his coloring make him a pariah among his peers or did something inside him, a feeling of uniqueness or the desire to be a loner, push him to the edge of his community? If he had been human, he might have chosen to live off the grid or explore the world alone, a backpack his only possession. The last time the cowboys and I moved the herd across the Little White, Happy meandered upstream, enjoying the fresh water. When I went to gather him, he willingly obliged, a twinkle in his eye and a grin on his face. "You're a funny guy," I said to him.

I revved the motor. Not too far from Happy, a gray mare lifted her head. "Watch her," I said to John the last time we moved the herd. "She'll know which gate we want to use." Before we even assumed our positions to round up, she started trotting toward the exact corner gate we planned to go through. Somehow the memo got to her early, and like an efficient manager, she got everyone up and going. If I could, I would have given her a raise. She made our job easy.

I took off down the hill. The horses started to move away from me like ripples in a pond. I parked the cycle near the fence and the ripples stopped. I had intended to putt through the herd, but the day encouraged me to stretch my legs and walk. The horses always appeared calmest when approached by foot, and I loved stepping into their world. It was like stepping into a friend's house. Furnishings, photos, colors can reveal otherwise hidden dimensions of a person. Even smells—of cats or dogs, of pot roast cooking or freshly baked pie cooling—speak to you. My boots treading the floor of the horses' home, their conversational snorts, grunts, and farts around me, spurred me through a portal into their dynamics. I felt the bonds between families and intercepted the glares between adversaries.

"Good morning," I said to a chestnut mare and her baby. Many of the horses were starting to put on summer weight. The meager grass clumps were evidence of their appetite. Horses ambled away from me, still shy or nervous. A palomino walked parallel to my path. I stopped to see if she would approach, but she wasn't quite

14. Settling in at Mud Lake

ready. I wandered through the maze of colors and battle scars, greeting the pretty and the pretty homely.

Not wanting to miss Alan Jr.'s arrival, I climbed back on the motorcycle and sat for a moment to let the experience imprint my memory. In the distance two coyotes slunk along the fence line. They wouldn't attack. They took the easy road. Wait for horses to die, strip the carcass overnight, and leave ghost-white bones behind. More than once, coyotes had devoured the hip where the BLM branded a number. We were required to remove this number from our master list and notify the BLM. In that case we could report only "one unidentified horse dead."

On Monday, Al started breaking Sally. I watched him ride her around the corral. Amazingly, she never tried to buck or run off like many a domestic horse would try doing. Although she didn't argue about having the weight of a man on her back, she looked a bit awkward and uncomfortable with him on board. After a few days, I tried riding her. She did okay. I thought maybe we could ride her occasionally.

Although Blue was as gentle to handle as Sally, she never followed us around the corral to be petted. Alan rode her twice. The day before he left, he walked into the corral and started petting her. He was standing by her shoulder and reached down to rub her belly. This must have startled her for some reason. Her hind foot shot up and kicked him with amazing force. Alan went sailing across the small corral. He never saw it coming and neither did I. He wasn't hurt, just stunned. He returned to Tucson the next day and no one ever finished the job of breaking her.

After he left, a bomb dropped.

Jerry Norbert phoned me that morning. "You know the Flathead Lake area of Montana?" he asked.

"Yes, I've never been there but hear it's a gorgeous spot."

Norbert said that someone in the BLM had decided to spruce up that area. The lake had a large island, named Wild Horse Island, and this dreamer envisioned making fishermen and tourists very happy by showcasing a painted mustang on the island.

Norbert said, "The trailer will pull up on Wednesday. Can you have Happy ready to load?"

All I could think of to say was, what in the hell are you thinking? So I didn't say anything. For a moment.

"Are you telling me you're deporting Happy to an island in some godforsaken northern part of Montana?"

"Ah, yeah. That's pretty much what I'm saying." Norbert sounded like he recognized the absurd in the proposition. Geez, how did he put up with his job?

I dug for information. Who thought this up? What was the BLM trying to accomplish? Were they going to take other horses away? He didn't know, or wouldn't reveal what he knew. I threw the empty shovel aside. By contract, the BLM had the power to do anything they wanted with the horses. They owned them all.

"I'll have him ready," I said, a cloud of shock descending.

"Sorry, Al," said Norbert and hung up.

15. Happy

On the appointed day, I loaded Happy into a BLM trailer. He didn't argue but, once inside, shook his head like he was trying to clear out confusion. Or maybe a bad memory of being shipped on the road. I hoped not. I wanted him always to be happy. Maybe going to a remote island was his destiny and he had been preparing for being alone while here at the ranch. Take it easy, I told the driver.

Years later I met some people who talked about fishing on Flathead Lake. I asked if by chance they had a seen a black-and-white paint, a big horse, on the island in the middle of that coldwater lake. They shook their heads no. Knowing Happy, he probably chose to hang out in the middle of the island as far away from humans as possible. For all I know maybe he's still hanging around. In my daydream, I envision him there, noble as ever.

Being different can bring you trouble or it can bring you rewards. I've watched it play out both ways.

I had just finished currying Aunt Jemima when Sarah came running into the barn.

"Dad! Dad! My friend Shelly called, and she's going to a really big regional jumping show in Salt Lake City. Can I go? I really want to go."

For the past few years Sarah had been competing in and regularly winning jumping shows in Arizona, but recently her twelve-year-old eyes had been searching for an advanced level of competition. Well, she had just found it. The show, however, lasted fourteen days. I couldn't take off that amount of time, which meant Sue would chaperone. After parental negotiations that went on for weeks, Sue and I figured out how to fit the trip into our schedule.

I had bought a bargain two-horse trailer for hauling Blondie and Squaw to the various shows. It was as beat up as the old pickup I drove around the ranch, a real Grapes of Wrath contraption with big patches of bare aluminum showing. I decided to paint the trailer to dress it up a notch. Bad decision. I knew nothing about painting vehicles. Since I didn't own a spray gun, I painted with a brush. Rather than restoring its original white color, I chose a dull blue paint. The thin paint dripped and ran. Every brushstroke showed, as did every dent, none of which I had bothered to fix. Rust marks and white paint peeked through the blue.

Sarah and Sue flew to Salt Lake while I trailered the two horses the twenty-four hours it took to drive there from Lazy B. I left at 5:00 p.m., drove all night, and arrived at 5:00 p.m. the next day. I pulled off the freeway to stop for fuel and to find a few ranch roads that had adjacent pastures where I could walk the horses and give them water. I met up with the girls at the hotel they had booked and turned the trailer and horses over to them. I had a lot of work to do at the ranch so the two of them had to deal with the show. I crashed for twelve hours before flying back to Arizona.

After the first day of the show, Sarah called, upset.

"Dad, all the girls here are fancy. Everyone drove up today in RVs that are as big as a bus and they live in them right on the grounds. And the trailers have all this shiny chrome and their horses are so pretty. They're almost all thoroughbreds, and they've been kept under the heat lamp all winter and have short, shiny hair and shellacked hooves. And Dad, the worst part is those girls are making fun of me." Sarah started to cry.

"Talk to me, sweetheart."

"When they saw our old beat-up pickup and ugly trailer and then Blondie and Squaw with their long winter hair, they started saying things like, 'Did you get your horses from Roy Rogers?' and then they started calling Blondie 'Trigger.'" Sarah choked back a sob. "Even worse, they made fun of Blondie's brand. Not one other horse has a brand."

When Allen Stratman delivered Blondie, he had already branded her quite prominently, and of course Squaw bore the Lazy B brand. "I know we're not going to win the hunter classes."

I could feel Sarah's pain. My mind raced, trying to think of the right words to offer my daughter. "Look, Sar, you know the hunter classes are beauty competitions. A pretty horse and rider with correct postures wins. You're entered because they're good preparation to get your jumping form right. But you went up there not expecting to win the hunter classes." Sarah sniffled in agreement. "The second week is the jumping competitions. I'm here to tell you that you're well mounted. Squaw is good in the large pony classes and Blondie absolutely excels in the open jumping. So you're going to have to bide your time until the jumping classes start. Hold your head up during the hunter contest and don't worry about the shiny horses winning. Your turn will come in the jumper division. That's the place where it matters how high you can go and how fast you can do it. Blondie and Squaw gave you their trust long ago and they'll come through for you. Just watch."

"Okay, Dad." Sarah's voice sounded a bit calmer. "I won't worry about the hunters."

"After it's all over, we'll have another conversation and I bet you'll see things differently."

16. Sarah and Blondie competing

The next evening the phone rang again. This time it was Sue. She was not a happy show mom. That morning, she and Sarah had driven the horses the eight miles to the show grounds. When the old trailer bounced across a set of railroad tracks, its floorboards ripped loose and fell to the pavement. Neither Sue nor Sarah was aware anything was amiss behind them. The only thing left to hold up the horses was the angle iron that held the boards. Fortunately, Blondie and Squaw's ranch survival skills kicked in and they managed to find some footing. If they hadn't, they would have fallen through to the pavement and been dragged along, even killed. I felt like a damn fool. What was I thinking when I bought that trailer? By the time Sue vented on me, she had already had the boards replaced.

On the last evening of the show, the phone rang with the call I was anticipating.

"Dad! Dad! I won the grand champion jumper award with Blondie and the reserve champion with Squaw. I had so much fun. And those girls who made fun of me were coming up asking where I bought my horses. I think we should come back next year, don't you?"

"I'm thinkin' so," I said, smiling. I couldn't have been a prouder dad.

CHAPTER SEVENTEEN

Sorting the Seven Hundred

The BLM called and said a rep from Washington DC would be out in two weeks to view the horses. Twenty-five years of working with the BLM had taught me that field reps didn't come from DC, bureaucrats did. I couldn't get any additional information from the person who called. Maybe someone in the hierarchy had decided it was time to find out what was going on at Mustang Meadows and learn a thing or two that could be used to help unadoptable horses in other parts of the country. Then again, maybe that was wishful thinking. The BLM had shifted its policy this way and that over the years, spinning the weather vane in all sorts of directions. I wasn't sure if the copper rooster would point north, south, east, or west. I guess I would find out when the rep showed up.

And show up she did, on the appointed day. I happened to be in the barn when I heard the crunch of gravel. I knew the Suburban was in the lot and John, Marty, and Russ out on horseback on the ranch. So it had to be her. A woman in jeans and boots, with a clipboard tucked under one arm, introduced herself.

"I'd like to take a look at your horses," she said.

"Not a problem. We can hop in the Suburban here and go out to the meadow."

I asked if she wanted a cup of coffee or lemonade first, but she declined, so we got down to business.

"You have a herd of fifteen hundred horses?" the rep asked.

"Yes, we've had that many for three years now."

She didn't ask the usual questions about the ranch. What's it been like to care for fifteen hundred wild mustangs? Can you train them? Did you have to change the ranch to accommodate them? Nor did she comment on how calm they were when we drove through the herd. Her comments were more like, "Stop here for a moment," and she would proceed to look in every direction and make notes on her clipboard. We spent a good two hours meandering the truck through the herd. She would point in the direction we should go. I'd see horses that I recognized. The big blue roan with only one eye and scars running down the left flank. The squatty chestnut mare, one of the smallest horses in the herd. And the palomino sisters. These were a few of the unadoptables that formed our family, and I couldn't help but be proud of all that we had done together. As we went along, I daydreamed. A couple of times I got out and pulled on the grass. I made a mental note to tell John we'd best move the horses in three days.

I wasn't paying attention when the rep said go to the left. I knew the ground there was soft because a spring ran nearby, and what did I do but drive right into the mud. I felt the truck sink. No way could I drive it out. I put my arms over the wheel and looked up at the bright sun above. Good thing it wasn't raining.

"Well, it's almost lunchtime," I said. "How about a little hike back to work up our appetites?"

On the way back, we small talked about her career with the BLM and a bit about the ranch and this part of South Dakota. John, Russ, and Marty already had arrived in the kitchen when we got there. They hadn't seen us walking in on foot. I told them about the Suburban getting stuck and said that I'd get a tractor out there after lunch and pull it out of the mud. We finished the sandwiches Debbie had set out before leaving to run errands in town.

"Anything else you'd like to see?" I asked the rep.

"No, I've seen all that I want to see. I do have a few more

questions before I leave." The boys took this as their cue to excuse themselves. She asked how difficult it was to handle the horses. Could we sort them easily? I explained we had them trained and yes, it was easy to bring them in and sort them. For a moment, I thought she might inquire as to how we had accomplished that feat.

Instead she said, "I want you to cut seven hundred horses. Cut the largest animals by weight and size. We'll schedule drivers to pick them up. Can you do that within two weeks?" Her placid expression seemed to indicate that this request was quite ordinary.

But I had just been thrown on the ground in a wrestling maneuver and had the wind knocked right out of me. I stared at the sweating glass of lemonade in my hand, stunned. This is what the BLM had in mind when they called?

"You want me to cut seven hundred horses? That's almost half our herd." She nodded. "What's the BLM going to do with them?"

"We're putting them in the adoption program."

The disbelief that flooded through me had to have registered somewhere on my face. Our horses had been deemed unadoptable. They were brought to us because no one wanted them. Many of our largest horses were scarred or crippled. They were not pretty horses. If they hadn't been adopted the first time around, they weren't going to be adopted the second time. Unless there was another reason. I took a sip of lemonade.

"So the BLM feels these seven hundred will be adopted?"

The woman sitting in the chair next to me nodded yes. Her expression remained steady.

"And it doesn't matter if they limp or are missing an eye or have scars all over? You want the seven hundred largest animals regardless of physical abilities?"

"That's correct."

"Regardless of color? Health? Looks?"

"Yes."

"You want the largest horses. The ones that weigh the most."

She looked down at her clipboard as if to check it and nodded. Right then I saw through it. Their transparent plan. It wasn't even cloaked in plausibility. Earlier in the year the price of horsemeat had taken a significant jump up to eighty cents per pound. If you adopted a horse, you couldn't legally sell it for a year, but after those twelve months you could sell it to whomever you wanted. As far as I knew, no one policed sales to make certain they didn't happen during that first year.

My mind scrounged for options. We had the first-ever government-sponsored wild horse sanctuary and were bestowed with the responsibility of caring for these horses. We had A ratings across the board. We had made improvements in the ranch to accommodate the horses and we were now operating a well-oiled machine. This didn't seem to matter to the BLM. Some people somewhere saw dollar signs and were making decisions. In my opinion, which didn't hold an ounce of water, they were the wrong decisions. The BLM owned the horses and could dictate what they wanted to do with them. I was landlocked here. I had nowhere to row.

"Circumstances sure must have changed for seven hundred unadoptable horses to now be adoptable," I said. If I had had eighty cents in coins in my pocket, I would have laid it on the table. As it was, the number hung in thin air between us.

"Can you have them ready for us in two weeks?"

I shook my head yes.

The rep pushed back her chair and stood up.

Her last words before climbing into her car were, "I'll have someone call you to schedule the pickups. I'm sure it will take some time to haul the horses out. I know the trailers only carry about thirty or forty horses."

"Forty," I said.

"Forty. That would be about twenty-six trailers." She was quick with math. She probably had already figured out that a thousand-pound horse at eighty cents per pound would bring in $800. Some buyers would be willing to pay the BLM's $150 fee for an unadoptable, wait a year, then sell their real estate to a slaughtering house for the $800. The BLM could get rid of horses, which they were always trying to do. The spirit of the law said horses couldn't be slaughtered and technically the BLM was honoring that spirit. But the veil was sheer. This was slaughtering with a straw man in between.

I watched her drive away. She hadn't been friendly or unfriendly. She was doing somebody's bidding, but I didn't know whose and suspected I never would. This was a huge shift in policy that would not receive any fanfare or public announcements. Perhaps if I were the muckraking type, I could dig around for a trail and go sniffing along it, then raise hell. But I preferred the smell of healthy green grass and the animals that fed on it. In my mind, the sanctuary was a permanent home for unfortunate horses. At the moment, though, it felt more like a pawn on the government's chess table. I shifted my thoughts away from the game and onto the needs of the horses.

I climbed onto the tractor and swung it toward the stuck Suburban. For the first time, I was glad that Happy was no longer here.

That night I talked to John. We had a new issue to face. In less than a day, our thriving, profitable ranch had lost 50 percent of its income. What effect would this have on our future? We needed to do something to keep the ranch solvent and running. We had the water tanks, windmills, grass, corrals — so much had been improved on the ranch.

"Maybe I could lobby for more horses," I said to John. He took a long drink of beer and shrugged his shoulders.

"I'm not sure you can count on the government to give you more. Seems like they've been taking away a lot more than they've been anteing up." He looked as skeptical as I felt. It was hard to dredge up the energy to think of dealing with the BLM to get more horses. "What about running cattle?" he said.

I had thought about this. We had a ranch designed for horses, but we could make some changes to accommodate cattle. We could replace the seven hundred horses with about one thousand head of cattle. Did I want to do that? Not particularly. Did I need to do that? The bottom line voted "yes."

It took us six hours to sort the seven hundred largest horses. Once that task was completed, we turned the remainder of the herd out in the pastures and kept the selected horses in the corrals until the BLM's two contracted trucks arrived. We'd load the trucks then wait for their return. It took seventeen loads and one month to haul them all away. The horses went out to five separate adoption centers. I never heard whether or not they all got adopted and didn't have the heart to ask.

I didn't call the congressional representatives who had sponsored our bill. They might have spoken to the BLM and objected to the whole thing, but I retained a sense of optimism. Time and again we'd proven ourselves good caretakers of the horses. If the BLM now had a better plan for caring for horses, I had no objection. I was interested in the well being of the animals, not in the underlying politics. For some reason, the BLM didn't take any of Dayton's horses. I never found out why.

Since the horse herd was cut in half, our ranch was now understocked. I couldn't get the BLM to talk to me about bringing us more unadoptable horses, so John and I started gearing up to bring in cattle. It's more difficult to run a ranch operation with two different types of livestock. When all we had was horses, we could focus on them at all times. Cattle need as much, if not more, attention than horses.

The eight hundred remaining horses still looked stately out on the pasture and I still loved them, but I could feel a hole, a disconcerting emptiness. I needed a friend. Aunt Jemima. She would be the perfect companion right now. I drove down to Lazy B, loaded her in the trailer, and hauled her up to South Dakota. I'm not sure if it was a good thing or a bad thing for her, but for me, it had the flavor of a family homecoming. I put her in a stall next to Clyde.

Marty took one look at her and said, "All your Arizona horses so small?"

"She may be small," I said, with a brush of irritation, "but she has a huge heart. Takes up half the space in her."

The South Dakota horses were bigger in every way, including having hooves like paddles that could ride the sand like snowshoes. Jemima's hooves, however, were made to traverse the rocky terrain of Lazy B. For her, traversing the prairie was like walking on a sandy beach. When she took a step, her hoof sank a good five inches. Pushing off the soft soil required different muscles and extra energy. Consequently, the other ranch horses could travel faster and farther. Although I couldn't take Jemima out on long days, we did quite a little work together on easier days.

Shortly after Jemima arrived, I purchased four hundred head of cattle. One day the boys and I rounded up a group of cows and herded them into headquarters. I was riding Jemima and she was happy to be in her element. We had pushed the cows against the gate and they were just about to go through it into the corral when a little doggie calf bolted away from group. We knew this little guy. His mama had died when he was quite young, and he had survived by sneaking up on nursing cows and stealing their milk. Often a cow won't pay much attention to a nursing calf, assuming it's her own. In this fellow's case, when the cow took notice of him, she kicked him away and wouldn't share her milk. The calf was smaller than he should have been, but he was a feisty little survivor. Before we knew it, he had run over to the swamp on the other side of the corrals and jumped in. He splashed out in the muddy water happy as could be.

Aunt Jemima saw the doggie turn out from the bunch. She just wasn't about to let that calf get away, so boy, she went right after him. She raced right up to the edge of the swamp and without a second of hesitation jumped in with me still in the saddle. Jemima swam toward the calf playing in the reeds on the far side. Her legs churned and she grunted. A big hump of grass stuck out of the water in front of her. Maybe Jemima thought she could get a foothold on it because she swam right up to it. Her momentum pushed her on top of the island and there she sat, high-centered and stuck, her circling legs unable to dig into the mud or propel her forward. I slid off and got wet clear up to my neck, but I was able to pull her off sideways and drag her to a place where she could get some traction. I was laughing and trying not to swallow water.

After all this commotion, the calf decided that he had had enough of us chasing him around so he splashed over to the swamp's edge and scrambled out. Aunt Jemima followed him and slogged out, dripping water. The cowboys witnessed the entire event and had a few remarks when I rode up covered in mud. I got a kick out of Aunt Jemima showing her big heart. She wasn't going to let that calf get away and would have followed him to hell and back. That was Jemima, though. She got the job done. That was our shared philosophy: you do what is required of you, even when you might not want to do it.

CHAPTER EIGHTEEN

Order to Kill

Rather than accompany John Pitkin out on the range after lunch to repair a windmill, I remained at headquarters. Jerry Norbert had called a few days before and scheduled a visit for 2:00 p.m. In preparation for today's visit, Jerry had asked me to identify the twenty-five horses that were oldest and in the poorest condition and pen them for inspection. It had taken half a day to drive our current herd of eight hundred horses into the corral, sort out the twenty-five oldest, and return the rest to the range. The BLM operated on shifting sands, so I had no idea what Jerry had in mind and he hadn't offered an explanation.

The day was chilled around the edges with a lackluster gray sky, normal for early November. A cloud of dust rising above the road signaled Jerry's arrival. I met him at his pickup to shake hands and exchange a few pleasantries.

"Let's go see those horses," he said.

We walked through the large corral, the red barn on our left, then through a second, smaller one and into a third, square corral about a hundred feet wide. I shut the gate behind us. Jerry eyed the horses. Their ribs rippled under scruffy and dull coats and hipbones stuck out. The average age probably hovered around twenty-three or twenty-four years. They were eating good feed, but due to lack of appetite or weakened digestion had started to thin. They were approaching the end of their road.

"If you don't mind, I'll drive out and take a look at the rest of the herd," said Jerry. I busied myself in the barn for the forty-five minutes he was gone. I had just finished brushing Clyde when he returned.

"Clearly, Alan, you cut the thinnest horses out," he said from the doorway, "just like we asked." I put the brush down, patted Clyde, and stepped out into brighter light.

Jerry looked back toward the penned horses a few corrals beyond us. "Now we need you to euthanize them."

I didn't move. Neither did my brain. It was trying to wrap around what it heard. I felt it resist like a horse resisting an open gate.

"Jerry, my contract with BLM doesn't call for me to be killing horses," I managed to say. This wasn't a mere shift. This registered as a major quake on the horse care Richter scale. I scrambled to maintain my footing. "Why don't we continue doing what we did last year? Let them die when nature calls."

Jerry rubbed one of his elbows. "My orders are to kill the oldest, thinnest horses," he said.

My conscience wasn't accepting his orders.

"Look, we had no problems last winter. What do we accomplish by killing these horses?"

"I was told to have you euthanize them. Life is no longer any fun for them."

What was running through the minds of these people? What right did we have to assume life wasn't any fun for them?

"I didn't have an issue the first year when your bosses said cut out the oldest and thinnest and give them extra care. We did that. They didn't have to compete with younger, more aggressive horses. Goddamnit, they stayed healthy all year." My voice was growing louder. "Then you tell me to cease and desist that game plan. So we treated all the horses the same and some of the old ones died. Okay, so Mother Nature won. I'm fine with that. She always wins. But now you want me to outright kill twenty-five breathing, living horses?"

Jerry nodded. "It's an efficient way to deal with them. There's no reason for these horses to suffer."

And here I thought giving extra feed and attention to the older mustangs was a kinder, gentler way of taking care of them.

"This sanctuary was set up to give comfort and care to the horses and treat them better than they were treated before. You're telling me to kill them. That's just contrary to the tenet of the whole sanctuary. I can understand euthanizing crippled horses or horses in pain. The quality of their life is questionable. But I don't know about arbitrarily playing God and killing horses just because they're old."

All I could think of was that they were taking me out of the care business and putting me in the kill business. It was like telling a doctor to kill a patient who hadn't requested to be euthanized.

"It's been decided, Alan."

A fly buzzed past my ear. It was too late in the year for flies to be out. It landed on my arm, and I watched it crawl, slow and lethargic with ugly black eyes. I brushed it away.

"If you want the horses killed," I said, my voice barely audible, "you'll have to do it yourself."

Jerry slid his cowboy hat back and looked me straight in the eye. "I have a long drive back to Sturgis. I'll be needing to leave now to get there by quitting time."

With that, he turned, exited the corral, clicked the gate shut, and walked back to his truck. If he had offered his hand, I'm not sure I could have shaken it. I stood there for a long time, watching the fresh cloud of dust rise above the road and resettle. Anger, frustration, and disappointment rose with it, but instead of dissipating like the dust cloud, they hung heavy in the bitter gray day.

Questions jammed my mind. How could I kill horses I had worked to save? Would I jeopardize the entire sanctuary if I disobeyed this direct order? Could I call someone higher than Jerry in the agency? Could I hide twenty-five horses and get away with it? My code of ethics insisted I honor the contract with the BLM. It also said to honor my contract with the horses. I couldn't do both. But how could I choose one?

When John rode up an hour later, I relayed the BLM's orders.

"You never know what's coming next from those guys. What in the hell are they thinking?" He paced in front of me. "For some reason, they can't see into the workings of this ranch."

We hunkered down in my office for a brainstorming session before dinner. We sorted through every option, spread them out like a deck of cards face up on the table. But no matter how we arranged them, we could never create a hand other than the one I had been dealt.

Megan came in to announce dinner and invite me to join the family.

"You're going to have to make up your mind on this one, Al," John said, standing.

I nodded in agreement. Megan grabbed my hand to pull me out of the chair, but a ball of resignation weighed me down. I gave her a hug and told her and John to go on to the house without me.

The question raged within me as to whether the BLM or I had the right to play God. Yes, a natural death might involve suffering. A thin horse could freeze in a blizzard or live with pain in its joints before dying in its sleep. Cruel, perhaps, but natural. Would it be right to shortchange that process? Our culture hadn't made it a policy to arbitrarily hasten the deaths of elderly human beings who could potentially suffer before dying. Why should we do that with horses? Old age is a part of life, and we were set up to assist the horses as they transitioned through that stage.

I turned these questions over and over in my darkening office.

The only thing I knew for sure was that I never assigned a job I wouldn't do myself. If I had an ugly job to do and I couldn't do it, it would remain undone, because no one was going to do it for me, including a vet, who would be at least a half a day away and would require the involvement of the cowboys. John was right. The buck stopped with me. I didn't want to involve anyone else in this dirty deed. It was my job and mine alone.

I never did eat dinner that night.

As dawn cast a dull light through the bedroom window, I listened for the usual sounds. There were none. The morning entered strangely silent. It had been a sleepless night, one spent wrestling with my conscience. Would I betray the BLM — my boss—or the horses—my charges? I awoke with a sharp urge to be done with this mission. I had not discussed this with anyone but John. Not Sue, or Alan Jr., or any other usual confidante. It would only have extended my struggle because, as John said, ultimately I had to decide how to handle this horrific assignment.

I pulled myself out of bed and dressed. From the front hall closet, I grabbed my rifle and stuffed a box of shells in my coat pocket. The rifle would be more accurate than the .357 Magnum pistol used for euthanizing a horse with a broken leg or one that was otherwise disabled and already lying on the ground. Then you're shooting from two feet away. These horses wouldn't let me get that close.

I walked the two hundred yards to the corral. No employee appeared. Why would anyone choose to be part of this? They would respect my decision no matter what I chose to do; they loved the horses as much as I did.

I opened the gate and stepped into the corral. The twenty-five horses were peacefully stirring and grazing on the hay we had fed them. They noticed my presence. Two of them moved toward me, then whinnied and snorted. These horses knew me. I believe they liked me. For certain, they had learned to trust me. I had, these past few years, learned to look away from their eyes. This was part of our secret language, our code of respect.

I stood among the chosen. They were old and thin, you betcha, but deserving this fate? I think not. I had signed on to save animals. My dreams did not include betrayal. I wanted this whole ordeal over.

The first one was a dun mare with a big head and several scars on her front legs. I cocked the rifle, looked her straight in the eyes, and shot her cleanly between them.

She slumped to the ground in one big downward motion. Blood flowed from the wound, ran across her nose, and dribbled to the ground. It stained the straw red. "Oh my God," I thought. "It's the same blood, the blood Wild Horse Annie saw on the pavement. Oh my God, what have I done?"

I froze in front of the mare's corpse, unaware that the loud gunshot had only slightly startled the other horses. I was surprised that they didn't skitter at the noise, but they trusted me. They went back to grazing, seemingly unaware that a horse had gone down.

What am I doing here? Why don't I save these twenty-four? Where could I hide them? Hide them from the assholes who ordered them dead. How ironic that this whole wild horse business was about me living my dream. In that instant I felt totally betrayed. What was I doing in this godforsaken place? My thoughts dodged past the events about to happen in the corral, ran around them like a cowboy racing around barrels.

"I hate these horses. I hate this ranch. I hate the government," I yelled as loud as I could.

Strangely, the horses remained calm. They trusted me and I was about to completely destroy that trust. They didn't know enough to be frightened. One began to slowly walk toward me. Was he my next victim? Oh my God, I thought, I can't do this. But here he came. One old, very brave, very stupid, wild horse. This was not my dream. This was a nightmare.

The other men knew what was going on and stayed away. They knew I would handle it. I needed one of them to walk in there with me and tell me it was okay, that I was doing the right thing. No one came. I stood up straighter. I aimed for his head and dropped him cleanly. Twenty-three more to go.

I stopped thinking.

I didn't pray.

I was there but I wasn't there.

I floated above looking down at the scene, saw myself sob and yell and curse. I yelled at those son-of-a-bitch good-for-nothing horses to stand still.

Then I methodically shot them all dead.

I walked straight to the house, put my rifle in the closet, and grabbed my keys. It was thirty miles to Valentine. Somehow I got there and did who knows what for a few hours until my senses came out of shock enough to return to the ranch. When I arrived I could plainly see the multiple furrows in the sand where the horses had been dragged with our tractor out of the corral and over the hill north of the ranch to the pit we had dug for the carcasses of horses that might die. Even though I had not told anyone to bury the remains, the employees knew what needed to be done and did the job. That day, the pit almost overflowed.

The ranch hands and I never discussed the incident. Even John didn't utter a word about it. I don't know if the BLM ever ordered other large bunches of horses to be euthanized, but if they did I wonder whom they recruited to do the job. I could never do anything like that again.

For weeks afterward I could walk, talk, work, and eat but my mind was numb. Colors appeared as mere shades of gray. I was just going through the motions of living. Inside my feelings were so large and raw I didn't know how to handle them.

Time is our friend when we feel sorrow. Events become less vivid as time passes and we can sometimes return to a level of normalcy. I finally stuffed the whole episode in a mental box and shoved it on a shelf somewhere inside me. It's still there and I open the box only on rare occasions. The pain that greets me still stabs.

I don't like to think about what I did. I try not to feel bad. I try not to feel guilty and I don't analyze. I just know that my dreams for the wild horses were diminished by the fate of those twenty-five. When I think back on the wonderful years at the sanctuary, this black memory hovers in the background like a cloud of unsettled dust.

CHAPTER NINETEEN

An Unlucky Penny

The stack of printed pages had to be six inches high. I carefully set it in the box Debbie found for me, then taped the box shut and wrote my name and address on top of it. I planned to leave tomorrow morning to deliver the package to the Bureau of Land Management's office in Denver.

It took three weeks to complete this project. Actually, it wasn't a project; it was a bid to keep the wild horses. The BLM had called to remind me that every four years the agency was required to rebid the sanctuary. Anyone with enough land and grass, the proper corrals, and handling facilities could submit a proposal to assume custody and care of the eight hundred horses living on Mustang Meadows Ranch. I hung up the phone baffled. I had assumed rebidding wouldn't be necessary. We ran a well-oiled operation that received the highest marks with every inspection. As long as we were doing an exemplary job, why change things?

John shook his head when I told him about the bidding. "Something's going on at levels we can't see. And if you can't see the problem, how can you fix it?"

The next day I hauled up to the BLM office in Sturgis for a face-to-face chat with the district director.

"I can't change government regulations, Al," he said before I had a sip of coffee.

"But you have a proven product with us. With someone new,

you won't have any assurances that the mustangs will be taken care of in the same manner." He shrugged away my cowboy concern. I tried stepping into his bureaucratic shoes. They pinched. "Think of the increased cost. The BLM has to pay to gather the horses, administer blood tests, vaccinate, and ship them to a new location."

"That's not the point."

"Look," I said, "I don't need to have a monopoly here. I would guess the BLM owns more unadoptable horses than they've shipped to me. Why not create other sanctuaries? Re-up my contract and add to it? There are more than a few horse people out there interested in having a sanctuary. I'd be honored to consult with someone on how to get up and running and train a bunch of horses."

In addition to the 20/20 segment, Mustang Meadows had been featured in a slew of newspaper and magazine articles. The publicity generated a steady dribble of visitors, mainly other horse lovers and ranchers curious to see our operation. Some stayed on the ranch for an hour or two, others for an entire day. They barraged me with questions about managing the horses and working with the BLM. A handful of people said, "How do I get one?" As far as I was concerned, anybody could lobby for a sanctuary.

My thoughts returned to the horses. "Moving the mustangs will traumatize them. We've spent four years working hard to minimize their stressors. My crew and I know these horses and they recognize us. We're comfortable with each other. Plus, the horses are even trained."

"I'm sure they could readjust," the director said.

Did this fellow have any idea how a distressed horse looked and acted? How different that animal was from a Happy or Blue or Sally? Why did the horses' welfare seem to matter least?

"It's such a waste to start at ground zero," I mumbled, mostly to myself.

The bidding process turned out to be more detailed and cumbersome than I remembered. I completed forms, obtained maps, copied records. I still had an unsettling feeling about the entire situation. An inner voice told me it would be a good idea to personally deliver the bid to the BLM office on the exact day it was requested. Hence the six-hour drive to Denver on April 3, 1993, deadline day.

The slate sky hung low over the Nebraska and eastern Colorado freeways. By the time I hit the outskirts of Denver, snow flurried and melted on the windshield. Eventually, after a string of wrong turns, I pulled into the BLM parking lot. I lifted the box from the passenger seat and walked into the procurement office. A secretary greeted me and asked how she could be of assistance.

"I'm delivering a bid for the wild horse sanctuary. I believe the official bid opening is today." I pushed the box across the counter toward her. She frowned.

"I don't think today is the bid date," she said.

"The rep I spoke with a few weeks ago said it was due April third."

"I think that date changed." The woman turned to another woman sitting at a desk. "Do you know anything about the deadline for bids on the wild horse sanctuary?" An uncomfortable feeling pooled in my stomach.

"I'm pretty certain it's later in the month." She started rifling through a stack of papers.

"Let me find out for sure," said the first woman. She grabbed the box and walked with it into a nearby office. Muffled voices filtered out. The secretary returned, box in hand. "The bid date was postponed to April thirteenth." She gave me a funny look. "Didn't you know?"

"No. I was never contacted." Red flags shot up around me. Warning. Danger. "Why didn't anyone contact me? I'm the one who has the horses!"

"I have no idea, Mr. Day. Maybe they did and you didn't get the message?"

The BLM knew darn well how to get a hold of me. For the first time in my life I couldn't think what to do or which way to turn. Something felt wrong. Way out of whack. Usually I could plumb my inner thoughts, dive down, and quickly find an answer suspended in my consciousness. But not this time. I stood at the counter, my mind paddling in circles. The woman looked at the clock.

"Well, I came all this way . . ."

I thought of the past month and the hard work that went into the bid, thought of the long drive here and the return drive facing me. Frustration and a sudden weariness took hold of me. The red flags waved wildly, but they appeared too far away to grab.

"I guess . . . um, do you suppose, well, maybe I could leave it here?"

"Absolutely, you can leave it here." She reached for the box. For a moment, both our hands held it. I let go.

By the time I merged onto the freeway, I regretted leaving that box. I was all but certain events were being played out behind my back. When the sanctuary was coming together, the BLM initiated conversations and meetings. They visited the ranch numerous times. Dayton and I had the lead roles in the performance. Even though we dreamed up the sanctuary and I provided land, cared for horses, trained them, and loved them, it was plain to see my role had diminished. I wasn't even an understudy. I felt like an extra, and a dispensable one at that.

And if that was the case, where would that leave me? I could wallow in self-pity and grief, wring my hands in failure, and view myself as a victim. But to what end? Rather than crashing to the hard ground, I had always opted for the soft landing. I could find a new project. Add to an existing one. Maybe a new adventure would surface. Mostly, I needed to believe that luck remained stuffed in my back pocket. *Land on your feet, big boy,* I lectured myself, *just like you've always done. Figure out what to do next.* I had six long hours to think about it.

John and I spent most of April 13 working the meadow—checking the circular sprinklers, spreading alfalfa seed. The shadows had lengthened by the time I stomped my boots on the doublewide's doorstep and headed to my office. Sure enough, the BLM had left a message. Colorado was an hour behind so the fellow who called would still be there. I plopped in my desk chair and dialed his number. A smidgen of hope struggled for air.

"Ah, yes, Mr. Day. Thank you for returning my call," said a deep, unfamiliar voice. "You submitted a bid on the sanctuary and as you know those bids were opened today. I'm sorry to tell you, sir, that the bid has been awarded to another party."

Even when you expect it, the worst can still drive a hard one-two punch. "How much was I underbid?"

The man on the other end cleared his throat. "You bid $1.15 per head per day. The winning bid was $1.14 per head per day."

I leaned forward. "I'm sorry. Did you say $1.14 per horse?"

There was a pause. "Yes, sir, I did."

It was like I stepped in a puddle with a live wire. That bid underbid mine by one penny per horse per day. "You mean to tell me that I lost this contract because my bid was one cent too high?"

I could hear papers being shuffled. "If you break it down, yes, that would be the case."

The thought slammed me: this is no coincidence. Was the BLM really capable of pulling such an elementary, stupid, transparent trick?

"Who got the contract?"

"The Tadpole Cattle Company."

"That's not a name I know. Where are they located?"

"Down in Oklahoma. John Hughes owns it."

That name I knew. Two years ago, Hughes had been one of those visitors to the sanctuary. We had spent a day walking around headquarters and driving out to look at the horses. I shared a lot of information about feed, grazing, and general mustang maintenance.

I even explained how we trained the horses and how they easily moved between pastures. "Hell, I have a feed truck," he said. "I could just bait them with feed and get them to move." He never directly stated that he wanted a sanctuary but he sure seemed interested. I didn't know anything about this man or his operation and certainly wasn't going to blame him for my predicament.

"Has anyone bothered to do the accounting on this? I've shipped cattle from Oklahoma before. The whole shipping process, including blood testing, vaccinating, and transportation, will cost at least eighty dollars per head. The government isn't going to recoup its cost for years." My mind reeled through the math. If the government saved $3.65 per head per year, it would take about twenty-two years to recover the cost of moving the mustangs. And this made sense how?

"We have to go by the bids, Mr. Day."

Fuming, screaming, reasoning—nothing was going to budge the fortress in front of me. I removed my glasses and rubbed my eyes. "Is there a way to appeal the decision?"

"You can write a letter."

I wrote down the address and hung up. The peachy glow of the sky muted the room. It was too dark to saddle Aunt Jemima. My heart wanted to ride her out on the range, find the horses, and tell them how deeply sorry I was. I had done the best I could do. My head intercepted. Before you fall to pieces, go find John and give him the news. I forced myself out of the chair.

The news didn't surprise John. "Like I've been telling you, Boss. Something is playing out that we can't see."

We were sitting in the family room. I set down the glass of scotch I had poured before coming over. "I just want you to know that we're going to continue as a working ranch. We already have cattle out there and we'll invest in more." Tomorrow I needed to say the same thing to Russ and Marty. Part of my job was to be a pillar of reassurance. Unfounded worry never helped run a ranch. "It's been a hell of an experience, but it's changing and I aim for us to change with it."

Debbie popped her head around the corner. "Guys, it's dinnertime."

While sitting in the bright kitchen with my adopted family in a place I deeply loved, seeds of cynicism sprouted. For the first time in my life, my belief in the government wavered. Up until then, I believed if you went about it right, a good idea could be planted, watered, and harvested. I had gone to Washington DC and witnessed that happening firsthand. I believed the role of government was to support its citizens, even if the two parties didn't always agree. Heck, I had dealt with bureaucrats throughout my working career, butted heads and argued with them, and still we shared a beer now and then.

Later that evening, in the dark solitude of the doublewide, the questions streamed in. What was the BLM's goal? Was there a payoff? Was there a friendship involved? Was this action intended to benefit them or harm me? Is that the way our wonderful government works for everybody or do they just handpick victims? Had I done something to piss someone off? Maybe the most recent incident with the BLM had influenced the playing field.

About eight months before, the director of the BLM's Sturgis office contacted me. Someone in the agency's hierarchy had come up with the resume-boosting idea of microchipping the wild horses. A microchip would be inserted under the skin of each horse. A scanner could read the chip and identify the horse by its number. When a horse died, all we had to do was scan the chip and make the appropriate notation on a master list. What a great accounting system.

"It'll be real effective in the field," said the director.

"Yeh, about as effective as pounding sand," I snapped. "Unless we find a horse on the day it dies, the coyotes will clean it to the bone. Are you fixin' for us to scan the coyotes' stomachs?

The director disregarded my question and insisted I could insert the chip at the same time I vaccinated the horses. It wouldn't take but half a day. Nope, that's not true, I countered. It would take a week of intense work because we would have to head catch each horse, shave the animal, insert the chip, and make sure the number on the chip corresponded to the correct horse on the master list. Sometimes horses that shipped from different holding facilities had the same number freeze branded on them. In order to make sure we were working with the right horse, we would have to read the description of the horse—its physical traits and approximate age. This took time. The horse could be in the chute for five or ten minutes.

Finally I said, "Okay, if you're not going to listen to reason, I'll do it. But I'm going to charge you $5 per head. My contract doesn't mention microchipping mustangs." The director argued, but I refused to give in on this one.

He relented. "All right, we'll pay you the fee."

The cowboys and I ramped up for the project. I hired extra hands to help, and the BLM mailed the microchips and scanner. It was five days of hard work, but we completed the job Friday afternoon. First thing I did after the last horse exited the chute was call the Sturgis office and confirm that all the microchips had been inserted and the master list updated. The director sounded pleased.

"How do you want me to invoice you?" I asked.

"Oh, we talked it over," he said, "and we decided we don't need to pay you on this one."

This guy just lit a match and was waving it way too close to a flammable tank. "What's your justification?" I asked.

"You had to vaccinate the horses so they were in the chute anyway. We don't think it necessary to pay double for work you're already doing."

I burst into flames. "This is not the way I do business. We've always been honorable with each other and stuck to our verbal agreements. You agreed over the phone to pay me. You know it and I know it. And if you'll take one goddamn minute to think about it, you'll realize it's pretty stupid to stiff me because there are ways of getting paid. I can stop reporting dead horses. Before you'll know it, I'll have a herd of twenty-five to fifty phantom horses that you'll be paying me for. Plus, I have the master list that matches each microchip to a horse. I'm the only one who has the list. But if you won't pay me, I might as well tear that list up, right?"

No answers were forthcoming; I was stonewalled and stymied. Why would an agency alienate the guy taking care of their property?

I ended up getting paid. My herd of phantom horses grew just large enough for me to recoup my fee. I hated playing the game that way, but I wasn't going to be taken for a ride. We kept the scanner in the range truck, though all it did was collect dust.

Did that incident inspire the BLM to move the horses to a different ranch? I couldn't make the call on that one. Perhaps the Oklahoma crew had more friends in the BLM than I did. My dealings with the agency occurred almost exclusively at the South Dakota level. Perhaps they lobbied their congressional representatives. Golly, should I have been doing that? Once Dayton and I had our contract and Mustang Meadows was receiving high marks, I didn't think future lobbying was necessary. If John Hughes won the horses by lobbying, I took my hat off to his ability.

I decided to bounce the situation off of Sandra. From the inception of the sanctuary, I had made it a point not to seek my sister's opinion or involve her in any of our escapades. She immediately knew my options of recourse. The government has a court of law, she explained, that hears cases involving inane bureaucratic maneuverings. If I sued the BLM and won, I might get the bid overturned and be able to keep the sanctuary. She could help me go about the process of starting a lawsuit if that was the route I wanted to take. I said I would let her know if I needed assistance.

I rolled around the option for a few days. Did I want to spend the next two or three years in court suing the hand that was feeding me? I had never sued anyone. There would be lawyers and fees, anger and negative energy. If I won and there were people who didn't want me to be in the sanctuary business, they probably would continue to try to make my life hell. Plus, by that time I certainly wouldn't have the goodwill of the BLM. I decided that I was far better off not to tangle with the government.

On June 30, 1993, the sanctuary contract officially transferred to the Hughes group in Oklahoma. On July 15 I mailed an appeal letter to the BLM. Two weeks later a reply arrived in the mailbox. It was dated July 27, 1993.

The U.S. Department of the Interior respectfully requests that the bid protest of Mustang Meadows Ranch ("Mustang") be dismissed summarily as untimely.

The protested Bureau of Land Management solicitation was issued March 8, 1993, with proposals due April 13, 1993 (copy enclosed). It sought a single facility with adequate carrying capacity to support approximately 2,000 wild horses. Those horses were being maintained on three sanctuaries, one of which was the protester's. Mustang submitted a proposal in response to the RFP (copy enclosed). A contract was awarded to Tadpole Cattle Company on June 30, 1993. Mustang protested to GAO on July 15, 1993.

Mustang asserts in its protest that the government will not realize a cost savings from the award of the contract and that the solicitation fails to consider the stress and trauma the horses would suffer during transport. In effect, the protester is objecting to the basic premise of the procurement—consolidation of the horses at one site—and to the evaluation factors. Since these matters were apparent in the solicitation, Mustang should have protested prior to the date for receipt of initial proposals,

17. Horses at sunset

as required by GAO's bid protest regulations. 4 C.F.R. §21.2(a)
(1). Instead, Mustang submitted a proposal and only objected
to the solicitation when it did not receive the contract. Because
Mustang failed to file its protest in a timely manner, we urge
GAO to dismiss the protest summarily, in accordance with 4
C.F.R. §21.3(m).

No one ever mentioned the regulation that required an appeal
be submitted prior to the bidding process. If I had known about
it, I would have written the appeal the minute I received the bid
solicitation. I couldn't discern whether this was an egregious over-
sight or a premeditated one. Or neither. Nor did I know that there
were three sanctuaries in operation. Dayton Hyde had one, but
we had contracted for the same eighteen hundred horses. Were
we considered two separate sanctuaries? And where was the third?
Had Hughes already been caring for wild horses? Or was some
other rancher doing that?

I had been cut out of the BLM's line of communication. At one time that line had been wide open and as a result, a wild horse sanctuary was born. Now I couldn't get answers to simple questions. I was on an island as remote as the one Happy lived on. The only thing I knew for certain was the time had arrived to say goodbye to the wild horses.